English for Emails

EXPRESS SERIES

Rebecca Chapman

OXFORD
UNIVERSITY PRESS

Great Clarendon Street, Oxford OX2 6DP

Oxford University Press is a department of the University of Oxford.
It furthers the University's objective of excellence in research, scholarship,
and education by publishing worldwide in

Oxford   New York

Auckland Cape Town Dar es Salaam Hong Kong Karachi
Kuala Lumpur Madrid Melbourne Mexico City Nairobi
New Delhi Shanghai Taipei Toronto

With offices in

Argentina Austria Brazil Chile Czech Republic France Greece
Guatemala Hungary Italy Japan Poland Portugal Singapore
South Korea Switzerland Thailand Turkey Ukraine Vietnam

OXFORD and OXFORD ENGLISH are registered trade marks of
Oxford University Press in the UK and in certain other countries

© Oxford University Press 2007

Adapted from *English for Emails* by Rebecca Chapman © Cornelsen Verlag
GmBH & Co. OHG, Berlin 2003

The moral rights of the author have been asserted

Database right Oxford University Press (maker)

First published 2007

2016 2015 2014
10

No unauthorized photocopying

All rights reserved. No part of this publication may be reproduced,
stored in a retrieval system, or transmitted, in any form or by any means,
without the prior permission in writing of Oxford University Press, or as
expressly permitted by law, or under terms agreed with the appropriate
reprographics rights organization. Enquiries concerning reproduction
outside the scope of the above should be sent to the
ELT Rights Department, Oxford University Press, at the address above

You must not circulate this book in any other binding or cover
and you must impose this same condition on any acquirer

Any websites referred to in this publication are in the public domain and
their addresses are provided by Oxford University Press for information
only. Oxford University Press disclaims any responsibility for the content

ISBN: 978 0 19 457913 1

Printed in China

ACKNOWLEDGEMENTS

Prepared for OUP by Starfish Design Editorial and Project Management Ltd

Artwork by: Phillip Burrows

Photography courtesy of: istock photo library

Cover images courtesy of: Corbis (main image/C. Devan/zefa; bottom left/
G. Baden/zefa); Getty Images (top left/John Lund/Sam Diepuis/Blend Images).

 MultiROM

English for Emails is accompanied by a MultiROM which has a number of features.

Interactive exercises to practise useful phrases, vocabulary, and communication through your computer.

Listening extracts. These are in enhanced audio format that can be played on a conventional CD-player or through the audio player on your computer.

Useful documents including an A–Z wordlist in PDF format that you can print out and refer to.

If you have any problems, please check the technical support section of the readme file on the MultiROM.

Contents

PAGE	UNIT TITLE	TOPICS	ACTIVITIES
5	**1 An introduction to emails**	The email screen Email structure Subject lines	A questionnaire Big Brother is watching ... and checking your emails
11	**2 Formal and informal emails**	Register Formal/informal phrases Abbreviations Correct spelling	Emoticons How important is accuracy in emails?
18	**3 Enquiries**	Writing and replying to enquiries The advantages and disadvantages of email Polite language	Email addresses & symbols The danger of viruses
25	**4 Requesting action**	Writing to colleagues Talking about deadlines and taking action Common verb–noun phrases	Acronyms and abbreviations To cc or not to cc?
32	**5 Exchanging information**	Informing and replying Colloquial phrases and contractions Quoting from previous emails Being diplomatic	An email quiz Over-quoting
39	**6 Making and confirming arrangements**	Typical phrases for making arrangements Prepositions of time Saying you're sorry	Domain names Have you been spammed?

PAGE	APPENDIX
46	**Test yourself!**
	You've got mail!
48	Partner A
50	Partner B
52	**Answer key**
59	**Transcripts**
61	**Useful phrases and vocabulary**

About the book

Over the last few years, emails have started to have a huge impact on our professional and personal lives. They often replace a telephone conversation or a letter and many of us have to deal with hundreds each year. Just as in a letter or a conversation, you need to remember who you are talking to so that your language sounds appropriate. On top of that they are very often in English, making it more and more important to be able to understand and reply quickly, efficiently, and accurately. **English for Emails** will help you do this.

Each unit of the book looks at a particular aspect of emails in terms of content, register, and language. Each unit has a **Starter** to introduce you to the theme of the unit and an **Output** where you can do more listening practice. Throughout each unit there is a wide range of exercises to help you practise and these can be done with or without a teacher. There is an **Answer key** at the back of the book so you can check your answers. When you have completed the whole book you can **Test Yourself!** with the crossword on pages 46–47.

If you have a colleague or a partner, you can do extra email practice using the Information files in **You've got mail!** on pages 48–51. When you go back to work, have the book handy so you can look up the key expressions in **Useful phrases and vocabulary** pages 61–63.

The **MultiROM** contains all the **Listening extracts** from the book. These can be played through the audio player on your computer, or through a conventional CD-player. In order to give yourself extra listening practice, listen to it in your car. The **Interactive exercises** let you review your learning by doing extra activities on your computer; this will be particularly valuable if you are using the book for self-study. There is also an **A–Z wordlist** with all the key words that appear in **English for Emails**. This includes a column of phonetics and a space for you to write the translations of the words in your own language.

1 An introduction to emails

STARTER

What do you think about emails?
Make a cross on the scale to represent how much you agree or disagree.
(5 = I agree 100%) (0 = I disagree 100%).

1 You need the same language skills to write an email as you do to write a letter.

   agree | 5 | 4 | 3 | 2 | 1 | 0 | disagree

2 If you can *speak* English well, you can write good emails.

   agree | 5 | 4 | 3 | 2 | 1 | 0 | disagree

3 One of the most important features of an email is the subject line.

   agree | 5 | 4 | 3 | 2 | 1 | 0 | disagree

4 Accuracy is still very important when writing emails.

   agree | 5 | 4 | 3 | 2 | 1 | 0 | disagree

5 Using the 'cc' option is a great way to inform others who are not directly involved.

   agree | 5 | 4 | 3 | 2 | 1 | 0 | disagree

6 One reason for emailing is to reduce the response time.

   agree | 5 | 4 | 3 | 2 | 1 | 0 | disagree

7 If you need an answer straight away, it is better to use the phone than send an email.

   agree | 5 | 4 | 3 | 2 | 1 | 0 | disagree

Discuss your answers with a colleague and/or check the key.

UNIT 1 An introduction to emails

1 Label the screen with the following English equivalents.

attachment • contacts • deleted items • drafts • forward • high priority
• inbox • outbox • reply • reply to all • send/receive • sent items • subject

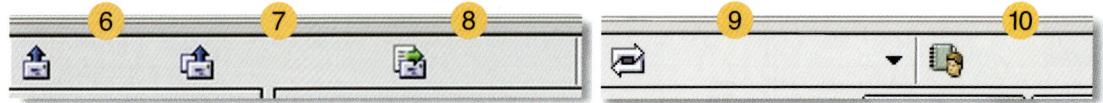

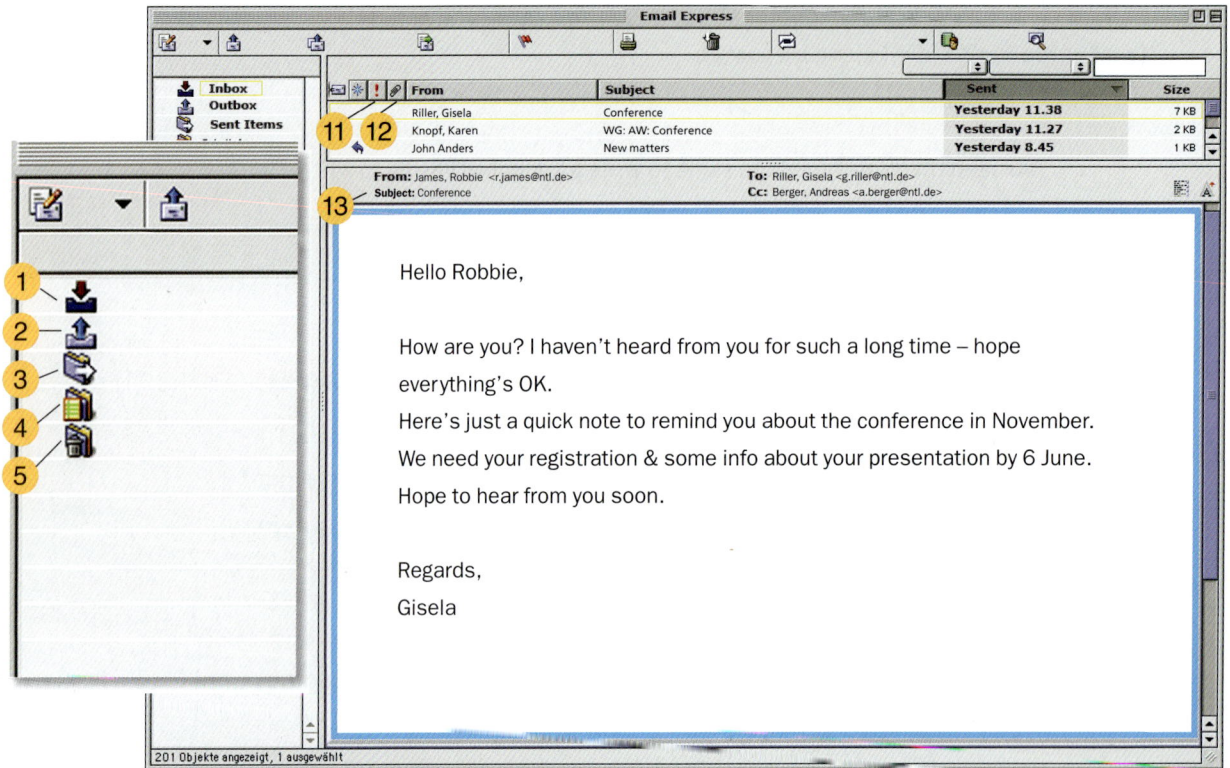

2 Where or how can you do the following?

1 Find old emails you have sent.
2 Find emails you have received.
3 Send an email you have received to a third person.
4 Find email addresses and other personal data.
5 Put emails you are working on but are not yet ready to send.
6 See what a message is about.
7 Show that an email is important and should be read immediately.
8 Find a document which has been sent with an email.

3 Now look at the message. Find five things that make it different from a letter.

UNIT **1** An introduction to emails | 7

 **Email structure**

One of the advantages of emails over normal 'snail-mail' letters is that they are quick and direct. We send an email for a particular purpose and we expect a fast response or immediate action. For emails – whether formal or informal – to be most effective, it is a good idea to give them a clear, logical structure.

Subject line: This should be short and give some specific information about the contents of your message.

Salutation: As in letter-writing, the salutation can be formal or informal, depending on how well you know the person you are writing to.

Dear Mr, Mrs, Ms …	*A formal form of address, also used when first contacting a person.*
Dear John	*Less formal. Either you have had contact with this person before, or they have already addressed you by your first name.*
Hi/Hello Mary (or just the name)	*Informal, usually used with colleagues you often work with. In the U.S.A. and the U.K. also sometimes used at first contact.*
(no salutation)	*Very informal, usually used in messages which are part of a longer email exchange.*

Opening sentence: This is used to explain why you are writing. (Remember: the opening sentence should always start with a capital letter.)

I'm writing to …	*More formal introduction to say why you are writing.*
Just a quick note to …	*Friendly, informal way to say why you are writing.*

Conclusion: This is where you tell the reader what kind of response, if any, you expect.

Looking forward to your reply.	*Friendly ending, can be used in formal or informal correspondence.*
Hope to hear from you soon.	*Informal ending to indicate a reply is necessary.*

Close: Like the salutation, this can vary from formal to very informal.

Yours sincerely	*Very formal, rarely used in email correspondence.*
Regards/Best wishes	*Most commonly used close, can be used in formal and informal emails.*
Bye/All the Best/Best	*Friendly, informal close.*
James/Mary	*Name only (or initials) is also common when writing to close colleagues.*

UNIT 1 An introduction to emails

4 Look at this excerpt from a typical inbox and find an email ...

from Martin which ...
1 is urgent.
2 is probably not work-related.
3 is asking for input.
4 contains new information about a meeting.
5 is a reply to an email you sent.

from Julia which ...
6 is a request for information.
7 was sent on from someone else.
8 contains one or several documents.
9 contains information about the new division.

INBOX

		Subject	Received
a	Martin Weber	ideas for a venue?	05.03.2003 12:34
b	Martin Weber	sales meeting	05.03.2003 13:36
c	📎 Martin Weber	something amusing for you	05.03.2003 13:53
d	Martin Weber	car park closed tomorrow	05.03.2003 15:34
e	❗ Martin Weber	sales meeting update	05.03.2003 17:41
f	Martin Weber	Re: tomorrow's event	05.03.2003 19:34
g	↩ Meadows, Julia	outstanding invoices	06.03.2003 09:02
h	❗ Meadows, Julia	FW: invoice 0167	06.03.2003 09:55
i	Meadows, Julia	REQ: current price list	06.03.2003 12:38
j	Meadows, Julia	Info	06.03.2003 16:49
k	Meadows, Julia	Info	07.03.2003 11:06
l	📎 Meadows, Julia	PET contract	07.03.2003 11:45

5 Did you have trouble answering number 9? That's because Julia's subject lines don't always give enough information about the contents of her emails.
Look at the following excerpts from emails and write appropriate subject lines.

1 Subject: _Production schedule_
Just a quick note to see if you've heard from Production about the new schedule. We need the info for tomorrow's meeting.

2 Subject: _XL20 motor handbook_
Many thanks for your email. The handbook for the XL20 motor is now available online at www.hardysgardensupplies.com.

3 Subject: _out of the office_
I will be away from the office from 3–5 October. Please direct all questions to Maggie in my absence.

4 Subject: _Time change_
I have to change our meeting to 3 pm instead of 12.00. Sorry!

5 Subject: _REQ: staff guidelines_
Could you send me those staff guidelines asap? Our dept hasn't seen them yet. Thx.

6 Subject: _Order confirmation_
I am writing to confirm your order of 1000 coffee mugs with logo (see attached), colour 32c.
Your order no. is 66193 F/2. Please quote this number in all future correspondence.

6

Look at the paragraphs below. Each paragraph belongs to either a formal or an informal email. Find the two emails and write the letters (a–j) in the table below.

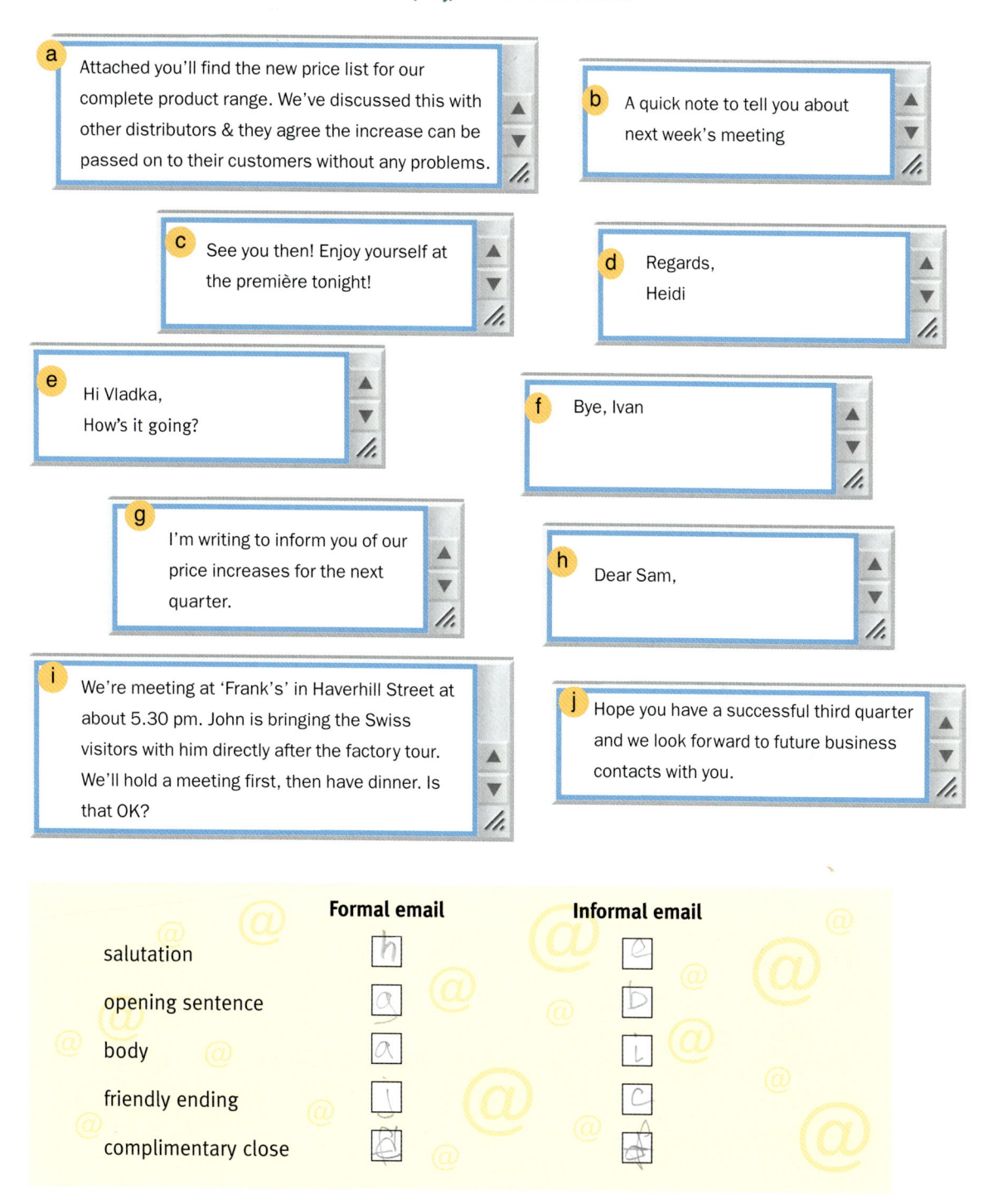

a. Attached you'll find the new price list for our complete product range. We've discussed this with other distributors & they agree the increase can be passed on to their customers without any problems.

b. A quick note to tell you about next week's meeting

c. See you then! Enjoy yourself at the première tonight!

d. Regards,
Heidi

e. Hi Vladka,
How's it going?

f. Bye, Ivan

g. I'm writing to inform you of our price increases for the next quarter.

h. Dear Sam,

i. We're meeting at 'Frank's' in Haverhill Street at about 5.30 pm. John is bringing the Swiss visitors with him directly after the factory tour. We'll hold a meeting first, then have dinner. Is that OK?

j. Hope you have a successful third quarter and we look forward to future business contacts with you.

	Formal email	Informal email
salutation	h	e
opening sentence	g	b
body	a	i
friendly ending	j	c
complimentary close	d	f

7 Use the clues to complete the puzzle and find the hidden word.

1. A typical email close
2. Where messages are stored before they are sent
3. What the email is about
4. To send an email you have received to a third person: to …
5. The opposite of *to send*: to …
6. What the exclamation mark (!) stands for
7. The text of an email
8. Another word for *answer*. Looking forward to your …
9. Where new emails go when you first receive them
10. Part of an opening sentence: I'm w… to let you know …

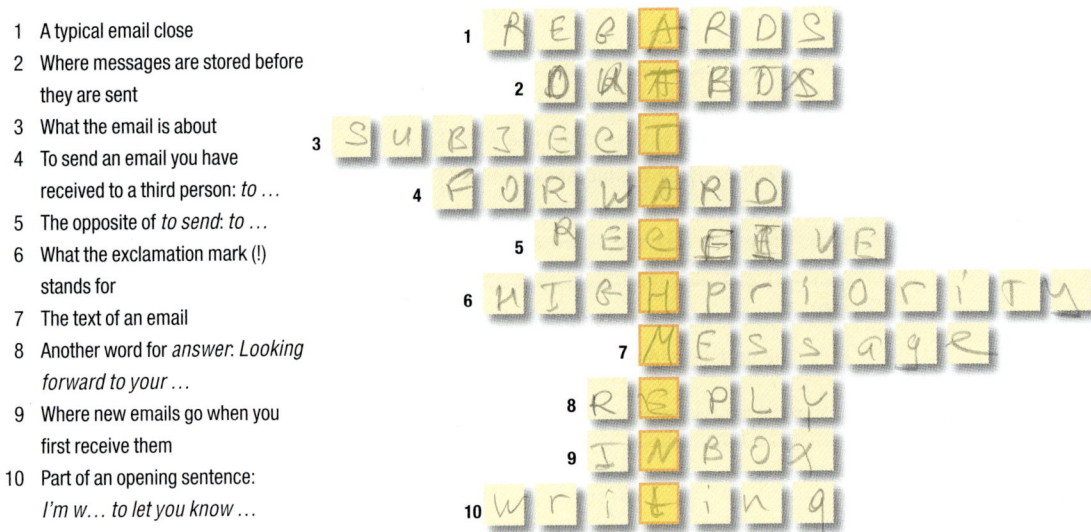

OUTPUT

Listen to this report and answer the questions.

1. What are large firms now doing?
2. How do employees react?
3. What are the main reasons for doing it?

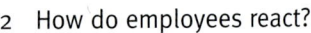

Listen to part of the report again and complete the missing words.

Lost _____productivity_____¹ isn't one of the main reasons for _____monitoring_____² e-communication, but some _____firms_____³ are worried that workers _____spend_____⁴ too much time using _____computers_____⁵ as _____toys_____⁶. 90% of workers say they _____receive_____⁷ personal emails during the _____work_____⁸ day.

OVER TO YOU

How much time a day do you spend on emails?
Does your company have an emailing policy?
Do you think companies monitor emails for security or legal reasons, or just to check on the staff?

YOU'VE GOT MAIL UNIT 1 Partner A page 48
                         Partner B page 50

2 Formal and informal emails

STARTER — Can you show emotion in an email? Match the emoticons to the correct meaning or description.

1	:-)	a	I'm angry or shocked (shouting face)
2	:-(	b	I've just made a sweet remark (face like an angel)
3	;-)	c	I'm happy (smiley face)
4	:->	d	I'm unhappy (sad face)
5	O:-)	e	No comment (neutral face)
6	:-O	f	I've made a joke or said something funny (one eye closed)
7	:-I	g	Sarcastic comment – more powerful than ;-)

Looks like someone's having a bad day ...

Now read the extracts below and add the appropriate emoticon.
(More than one answer is possible.)

8 Have a nice weekend!

9 You're great! Thanks so much for helping. What would I do without you?

10 Have you heard Paula's leaving the company & moving to the competition?!

11 My computer crashed yesterday & I lost all my data!

12 I don't believe you're finally going on holiday. In fact, I didn't think you even knew what a 'holiday' was!?

13 You're going to the conference with Steve. Do you know what he's like!?

14 Sorry, I can't talk about that! Top secret!

12 UNIT **2** Formal & informal emails

1 Look at the emails a – f. Which messages are formal and which are informal?

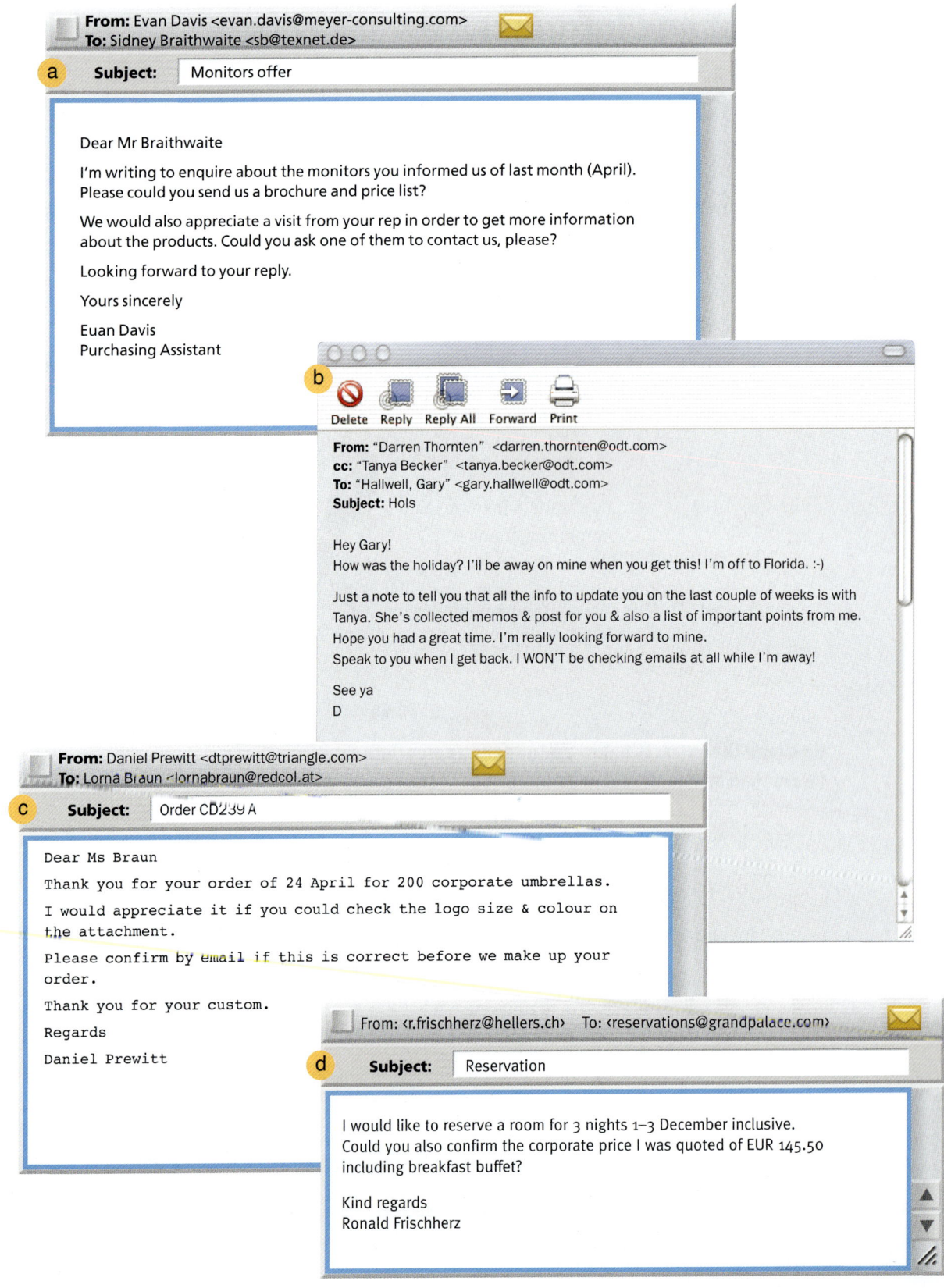

a
From: Evan Davis <evan.davis@meyer-consulting.com>
To: Sidney Braithwaite <sb@texnet.de>
Subject: Monitors offer

Dear Mr Braithwaite

I'm writing to enquire about the monitors you informed us of last month (April). Please could you send us a brochure and price list?

We would also appreciate a visit from your rep in order to get more information about the products. Could you ask one of them to contact us, please?

Looking forward to your reply.

Yours sincerely

Euan Davis
Purchasing Assistant

b
From: "Darren Thornten" <darren.thornten@odt.com>
cc: "Tanya Becker" <tanya.becker@odt.com>
To: "Hallwell, Gary" <gary.hallwell@odt.com>
Subject: Hols

Hey Gary!
How was the holiday? I'll be away on mine when you get this! I'm off to Florida. :-)

Just a note to tell you that all the info to update you on the last couple of weeks is with Tanya. She's collected memos & post for you & also a list of important points from me. Hope you had a great time. I'm really looking forward to mine.
Speak to you when I get back. I WON'T be checking emails at all while I'm away!

See ya
D

c
From: Daniel Prewitt <dtprewitt@triangle.com>
To: Lorna Braun <lornabraun@redcol.at>
Subject: Order CD239 A

Dear Ms Braun
Thank you for your order of 24 April for 200 corporate umbrellas.
I would appreciate it if you could check the logo size & colour on the attachment.
Please confirm by email if this is correct before we make up your order.
Thank you for your custom.
Regards
Daniel Prewitt

d
From: <r.frischherz@hellers.ch>   To: <reservations@grandpalace.com>
Subject: Reservation

I would like to reserve a room for 3 nights 1–3 December inclusive.
Could you also confirm the corporate price I was quoted of EUR 145.50 including breakfast buffet?

Kind regards
Ronald Frischherz

UNIT **2** Formal & informal emails | 13

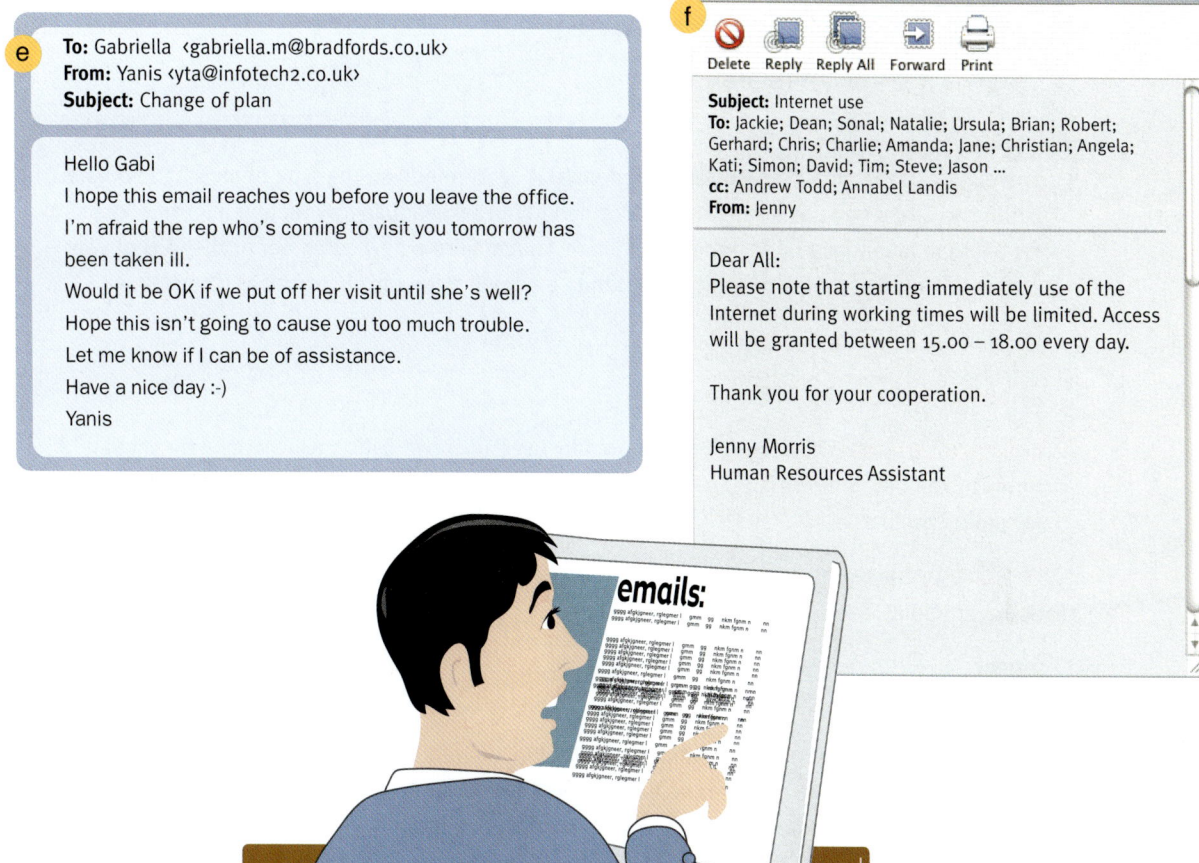

e
To: Gabriella <gabriella.m@bradfords.co.uk>
From: Yanis <yta@infotech2.co.uk>
Subject: Change of plan

Hello Gabi
I hope this email reaches you before you leave the office.
I'm afraid the rep who's coming to visit you tomorrow has been taken ill.
Would it be OK if we put off her visit until she's well?
Hope this isn't going to cause you too much trouble.
Let me know if I can be of assistance.
Have a nice day :-)
Yanis

f
Subject: Internet use
To: Jackie; Dean; Sonal; Natalie; Ursula; Brian; Robert; Gerhard; Chris; Charlie; Amanda; Jane; Christian; Angela; Kati; Simon; David; Tim; Steve; Jason ...
cc: Andrew Todd; Annabel Landis
From: Jenny

Dear All:
Please note that starting immediately use of the Internet during working times will be limited. Access will be granted between 15.00 – 18.00 every day.

Thank you for your cooperation.

Jenny Morris
Human Resources Assistant

2 Now look at the emails again and find the following.

1 An announcement to the staff of a new regulation
2 A message to a colleague
3 A message to a customer about a change in plans
4 A request for confirmation of an order
5 A hotel reservation
6 An enquiry to a supplier

UNIT 2 Formal & informal emails

> **TIP** **Register**
>
> The register of an email (how formal or informal it is) depends on the type of message you are writing and who you are writing to. So an email about rescheduling a meeting might be less formal than an enquiry or an apology. Similarly, an email to a new customer or the CEO of your company would probably be more formal than an email to an old customer or a colleague.
>
> You can tell how formal an email is by its …
>
> **Salutation & close:** See **TIP** on page 7.
>
> **Colloquial phrases:** These are phrases normally used in conversation which make an email less formal. Examples are *How's it going?* for *How are you?* or *See ya* for *See you later*. See page 34 for more examples.
>
> **Vocabulary:** The words and expressions used in an email can make it formal or informal. Some examples are:
>
> | | | | | |
> |---|---|---|---|---|
> | **formal** | to receive | to inform | to assist | to contact |
> | **less formal** | to get | to tell | to help | to get in touch |
>
> **Abbreviations:** The use of abbreviations and symbols (*eg* for *for example*, *info* for *information* and *&* for *and*) are more common in informal emails, although some standard abbreviations used in letter-writing – like *asap* – are also found in formal emails.
>
> **Emoticons:** These written forms of body language or gesture are often used in less formal emails to help the recipient understand exactly what you mean.

3 Find examples in the emails on pages 12 and 13 to complete the table.

	More formal	Less formal (or informal)
salutations & closes	*Dear Mr Braithwaite*	*Hey Gary!*
phrases & vocabulary	*inform*	*Just a note to tell you …*
abbreviations, etc.		*:-)*

4 Match the vocabulary used in formal emails (1–10) with the less formal vocabulary below.

> to answer • to ask • to get in touch with • help • to need • ok
> • to put off • to be sorry • to set up • to tell

1	convenient	=	OK	6	to contact	=	_____
2	assistance	=	_____	7	to postpone	=	_____
3	to inform	=	_____	8	to arrange	=	_____
4	to reply	=	_____	9	to enquire	=	_____
5	to regret	=	_____	10	to require	=	_____

5 Now complete the emails below with words from above. Be careful of the register!

1 Dear Mr Bass

I am writing to _____ [1] about your range of less exclusive products.

Our company has diversified recently and, in addition to the professional equipment we have previously purchased, we now _____ [2] products for the hobby golfer.

Could we _____ [3] a meeting to see one of your sales reps who can _____ [4] us about your products? The week of 19 August would be _____ [5] for us.

As I will be out of the office from 2 to 6 August, please _____ [6] my assistant, Sylvie Jouet, directly.

Best regards
Simon Pilgrim

2 Hi Sylvie

Just a quick note to say we are very _____ [7] for the delivery delay.

I'm afraid we'll have to _____ [8] the delivery date for 10 days because of the truck drivers' strike.

When exactly do you _____ [9] the goods? If it's very urgent I'll _____ [10] the manager of the forwarders whether we can _____ [11] a special delivery somehow.

I'll _____ [12] asap, but please let me know the latest date for the goods.

Despite this, have a nice day!
Rgds
Jean

UNIT 2 Formal & informal emails

6 What do you think the following abbreviations stand for? Write out the full meaning.

1. ie — in other words
2. asap — _____
3. Thurs — _____
4. Jan — _____
5. at the mo — _____
6. bw — _____
7. attn — _____
8. rgds — _____
9. pls — _____
10. w/e — _____

7 Read the two emails below and find at least five things that make them either formal or informal. Then use the notes to write responses in the right register.

Hi Johannes!

I'm coming over to Bern for a conference in 2 weeks & was wondering if you could sort out somewhere for me to stay? I've got a bit of info about the conference hotel, it's the Hotel Bern in Viktoriastrasse 43, but not sure I want to stay there! Can you help me pls?

Hope this is OK with you!

Teresa
PS How about meeting up for a drink one night? ;-)

- send map of Bern as attachment
- list of guest houses and hotels at <www.berncityscope.ch/accommodation.htm>
- dinner instead?

Dear Johannes

I'm writing to you about my visit to Bern. I'm attending a conference on 20 March and hope you can assist me in arranging accommodation. I've tried the tourist information office but they weren't very helpful.

The conference hotel is Hotel Bern in Viktoriastrasse 43 but I'd prefer to stay in a smaller guest house in the vicinity. Unfortunately I don't know Bern so it's rather difficult to find out where the best accommodation is.
I really hope the above is convenient.
Best regards
Sandy

- list of guest houses and hotels at <www.berncityscope.ch/accommodation.htm>
- can book online or should I book something?
- can recommend 'Pension Bergland' (my parents stayed there)

UNIT **2** Formal & informal emails | **17**

8 **Find ten spelling mistakes in the first email. Then correct the second email.
How many mistakes can you find? (Look out for punctuation too!)**

> Hi Charlotta
> Jsut a quik note to telll you that the info fort
> he new product has finally arrived.
> Ill get in tuch with you next week to update
> you on tormorow#s meeting in Romania.
> Can you put of the product mailing until I'm
> back?
> Seeyou soon.
>
> Ragrds
> Tibor

> Deer Mahendra
> we are still wating for the above oerder but have
> recieved no email to explain the reason for the deley.
> This is particularly inconvenient for us at the moment
> as as our clients need the dylivery asap
> Please can you kontakt the forwarders find out what
> has happened and inform us immediately.
> we look forward to hearing from you very soon
>
> kind regards
> Mia

OUTPUT

AUDIO 4

How important is accuracy in emails?

You will hear five people talking about emails. What is the main point each speaker makes? Note any important words they use.

 **Speaker 1**
_____
_____
_____

 **Speaker 2**
_____
_____
_____

 **Speaker 3**
_____
_____
_____

 **Speaker 4**
_____
_____
_____

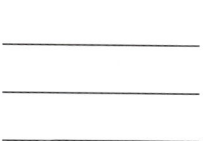 **Speaker 5**
_____
_____
_____

Which opinion do you agree with?

OVER TO YOU

How would you react if you received an email full of mistakes from someone you didn't know?
Would it matter if the person wasn't writing in his or her native language?

YOU'VE GOT MAIL ▶ UNIT 2   Partner A   page 48
                            Partner B   page 50

3 Enquiries

STARTER

Can you say your email or website address?
Match each symbol with how you say it.

at • back slash • capital 'h' • dot
• hyphen/dash • slash • small 'h'
• underscore

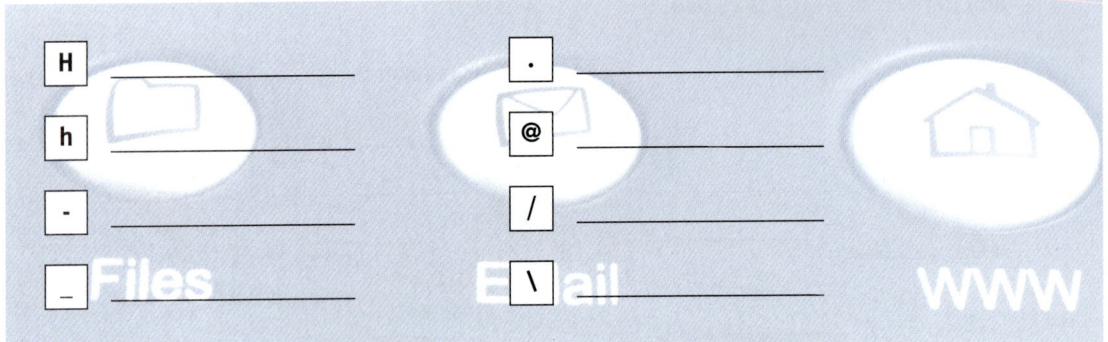

H	_____		.	_____
h	_____		@	_____
-	_____		/	_____
_	_____		\	_____

Now work with a partner. One of you look at page 51, the other look below.
Take turns dictating the email and website addresses to each other, then check your answers.

dictate

1 jason.carter@gmv.de
2 h.marlow@freeserve.com
3 p-onigl@fib.si
4 www.beat_top.com
5 geoff@hmj.ch

write

6 _____
7 _____
8 _____
9 _____
10 _____

UNIT **3**   Enquiries   **19**

1 Look at the ads below. Would you contact the companies by email, phone, fax, or letter? What are the advantages/disadvantages of contacting the companies by email?

Net-train
Computer / Internet training

267 London Road
Norwich
Norfolk
NR35 6QY
Tel. no. 01603 5167421
Fax no. 01603 6177421
email: training@net-train.co.uk
www.net-train.co.uk

HOTEL FALKENBERG

WANTED!
We are looking for a highly qualified receptionist to join our team in a 5-star conference hotel. Position available from April 1.
For further info contact: Sussie Karlsson, Personnel Manager

Box: 572
SE-31123 Falkenberg
Tel: +46 (0)346-166 50
Fax: +46 (0)346-166 58
s.karlsson@swedenhotels.se
www.hotelfalkenberg.se

All correspondence and applications in English, please.

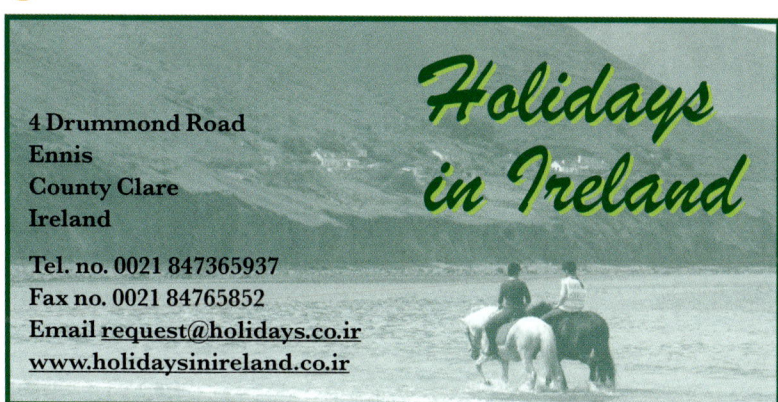

Holidays in Ireland

4 Drummond Road
Ennis
County Clare
Ireland
Tel. no. 0021 847365937
Fax no. 0021 84765852
Email request@holidays.co.ir
www.holidaysinireland.co.ir

2 Look at these parts of an email requesting information about the training courses in the first advertisement. Connect the sentences and put them in the correct order.

1 I am interested in ...
2 I look forward to ...
3 Could you please send me ...
4 I saw your advert in ...

a ... information on the length, cost, and contents?
b ... the *Financial Times* of 5 January.
c ... hearing from you soon.
d ... your Internet training courses.

Use similar phrases to write a short request to advertisement 2 or 3.

UNIT 3 Enquiries

3 Complete the table with the phrases below.

> Can you help? • We hope you are happy with this. • Let us know if you need any more help.
> • Please answer asap. • I'm sending you the … in an attachment. • I'm sending you …
> • Thanks for choosing … • We are working on your request. • Can you please send me … ?
> • Thanks for your email/request.

More formal	Less formal
Requesting information	
I'd appreciate a reply asap.	1 _____
Would you be able to help … ?	2 _____
Could you please send me … ?	3 _____
Replies	
Please find the … in an attachment.	4 _____
I'm pleased to send you …	5 _____
Thank you for your email/enquiry.	6 _____
Do not hesitate to contact us if you require further assistance.	7 _____
We hope you find this satisfactory.	8 _____
Thank you for your interest.	9 _____
Your request is being processed.	10 _____

4 Use (parts of) the phrases in exercise 3 to complete the request and reply emails below.

From: rachel.beamish@wells.co.uk   To: request@changingrooms.co.uk

Subject: Request for brochures

Our company is currently looking for accommodation for some overseas colleagues who will be transferred to Southampton for 12 months. _____¹ me some brochures showing the various houses and flats you have to offer. We also need to find locations near schools; _____²?
As our employees are arriving next month, I _____ _____³.
Thank you very much.

Best regards
Rachel Beamish
HR assistant
Wells Ltd

From: Brian Pearson <Brian@changingrooms.co.uk>   **To:** rachel.beamish@wells.co.uk

Subject: Re. Request for brochures   **Attachment:** Southampton.pdf

Dear Ms Beamish

_____⁴. Unfortunately, the brochure you requested is being reprinted at the moment, but _____⁵. Prices and location have remained the same, however, so you'll find the requested information _____⁶. The new brochure will be sent by post as soon as it's available.

We _____⁷.

_____⁸.

Regards

Brian Pearson
Relocation Specialist
Changing Rooms
Brian@changingrooms.co.uk
www.changingrooms.co.uk

TIP — Polite language

Even in informal emails, it is important to use polite language.
Please can be used in every type of request, and phrases with **could** and **would like** are more polite than phrases with **can** or **want**.

Could you please send me …   *Can you please send me …*
I would like to order …   *I want to order …*

In enquiries it is best to avoid imperatives like *Send me …* or *Inform me …*. By adding **please** the sentence becomes more polite, but is still rather direct.

Please send me your current price list …
Please give us your rates …

The following phrases can be used in formal enquiries to first-time contacts. However, they can sound too formal in emails to colleagues.

We would be grateful if you could send us …
We would also appreciate some information on …

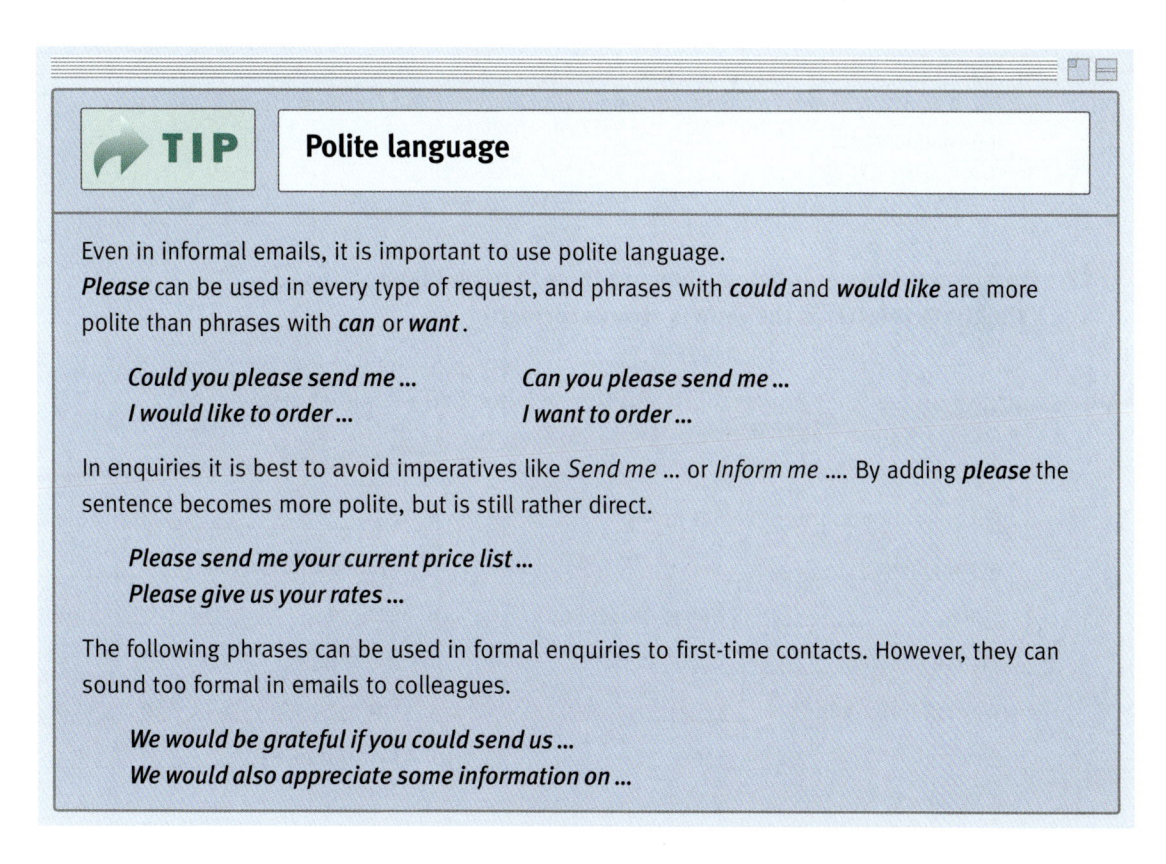

22 | UNIT 3 Enquiries

5 Rewrite these emails to make them polite.

> Our general manager saw your advert in yesterday's *Financial Times* and wants the free start-up packet advertised.
> Send it to:
> …
> We also want all the information you can send us on your after-sales service.
> Thanks in advance.
> T. Gerald

> Dear Giovanni
> Jane at headquarters gave me your name and said you will help me. I need some information about the upcoming trade fair in Milan.
> 1) Who is attending from the Milan office?
> 2) How many hotel rooms have you booked?
> 3) What time and where is the Tuesday night reception?
> Send me the information immediately.
> Regards
> Martin
> PS I want you to send me your extension number too. I can't find it on the international list.

6 Unscramble the words below, then use them to complete the gaps.
(Tip: the first letter of the word is always correct!)

> apsa • arppctieae • antttmance • eqyuirn • iertentsed • kwon • rqtseue
> • rvceiee • snde • stfcrisaatoy

1. I'm sending you the price list in the _attachment_ .
2. Your _____ is being processed.
3. Please answer _____ .
4. We hope you find this _____ .
5. Can you _____ me … ?
6. I'd _____ a reply asap.
7. Thank you for your _____ .
8. Let me _____ if you need any more help.
9. I'm _____ in … .
10. I would like to _____ … .

7 Use the information below to write an enquiry.

You are the sales rep for Bigtop electric drills and saws.
Write to James Baker (your colleague Sarah Miller gave you his name) to order some brochures on Bigtop's after-sales service. You need the English version of the brochures for a trade fair in the Czech Republic. The trade fair is next week!

UNIT **3** Enquiries | **23**

8 You receive the two enquiries below. Use your notes to write the replies.

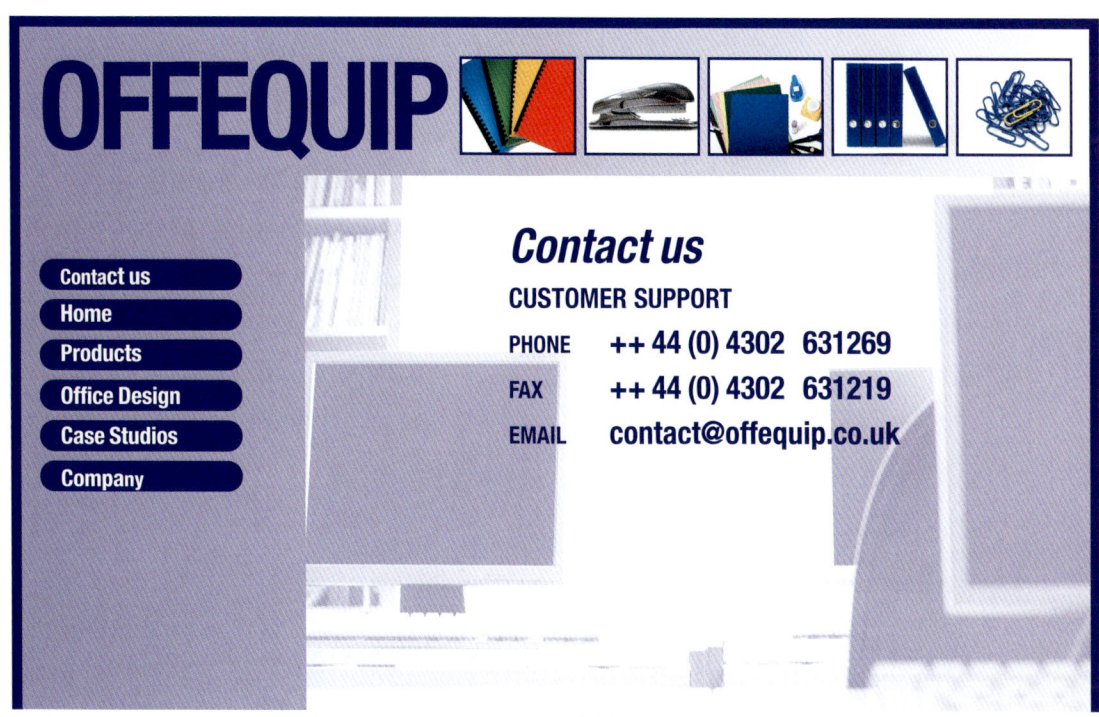

To: contact@offequip.co.uk
From: pia@vml.nl
Re: office furniture 'progress'

We are a medium-sized engineering company in Amsterdam and are interested in your 'progress' range of office furniture.
Could you please send us a catalogue and a current price list?
As we are in the process of deciding on office furniture for our new building, I'd appreciate a prompt reply.

Thank you for your help.

Pia Stevens

V.M.L. BV
Keizersgracht 384
Amsterdam 1016GB
Netherlands
Tel: +31 20 5 30 20 10
Fax: +31 20 5 30 20 30
e-mail: pia@vml.nl
website: www.vml.nl

package sent this morning, also attached as PDF file

To: contact@offequip.co.uk
From: sandy.adams1@web.fr
Re: info

Hello
I saw your website and would like to know where I can find your furniture in the Paris area. Also, can you please send me a catalogue?
My address is
Gérard Latour
54, The Royale
75012 PARIS

Thanks!
G. Latour

*list attached with shops and addresses
catalogue sent by post this morning*

OUTPUT

Read these two scenarios and answer the questions.

Scenario 1
You receive an email from an unknown company. Nothing unusual about that. You receive enquiries every day. But this one has the subject line:
I LOVE YOU. What do you do?

Scenario 2
You receive an email from a friend you haven't heard from in years and it includes a very short impersonal message and an attachment? Do you open the attachment or delete it?

Now listen to this report and answer the questions below.

1. What steps can you take to protect computers from viruses?
2. What about email attachments?
3. Is this a new phenomenon?

OVER TO YOU

Has your computer ever had a virus? Tell your colleague what happened.
What steps does your company take to protect against viruses?

YOU'VE GOT MAIL ▶ UNIT 3   Partner A page 48
                                    Partner B page 50

4 Requesting action

STARTER Emails – especially those from native speakers of English – can contain a lot of acronyms and abbreviations. How many do you know? If you have trouble finding the answers, look at the clues below.

1	Thx _____	7	Rgds _____
2	Tia _____	8	BTW _____
3	Re _____	9	Fwd _____
4	FAQ _____	10	REQ _____
5	CU _____	11	IMO _____
6	FYI _____	12	ATB _____

Clues

1 You write this to someone who has helped you.
2 You write this to someone who is going to help you.
3 This is used in the subject line and in the body of an email and means 'about'.
4 You see this on websites to give more information on the typical things people ask about.
5 You write this at the end of your email.
6 You write this to show no reply is necessary.
7 This is the short form of a common close.
8 You write this when you want to give some additional information.
9 You do this when you send the same email on to another colleague.
10 You write this when you want someone to do something for you.
11 You write this when you want to say what you think.
12 You write this as a close, to wish someone well.

The use of abbreviations and acronyms is not the only way native speakers try to keep their messages short. They often also omit articles, pronouns, or auxiliary verbs. Look at these sentences and write them out in full.

1 Looking fwd to seeing u next wk.
2 Tia for yr help.
3 Will be in touch tomorrow with updated figures.
4 Pls call me re our meeting on Thurs am.
5 Just a quick email to give you new dates.
6 Got any exciting plans for the w/e?
7 No info on pay rises at the mo. Hope to hear sth soon though.

UNIT 4 Requesting action

1 Read the two emails below and answer the questions.

1 What tasks would Simon like Pascal, Barbara, and Thilo to do?
2 Which tasks have been completed and who did them? What problem has this person had?
3 What do you think the working relationship is between the four colleagues?

a

From: Simon <swo@tdo.com>
To: Pascal <pbe@tdo.com>, Barbara <baz@tdo.com>, Thilo <thr@tdo.com>
Subject: quarterly sales reports

Hi all

I'd like you to send me the figures from the last quarter by tomorrow morning first thing. Pls let me know if you have a problem with this deadline.

Pascal: Have you coordinated your team & their results yet? Can you send the report to me by Thurs 4th?

Babs: Have you finished your sales report yet? By Tues 2nd June pls.

Thilo: Have you contacted Hungary about the new account details? Gerry needs this info asap.

Please reply asap.
Best wishes
Simon

b

From: Pascal <pbe@tdo.com>
To: Simon <swo@tdo.com>
cc: Barbara <baz@tdo.com>, Thilo <thr@tdo.com>
Subject: re quarterly sales report
Attached: sales_div2_1quart.xls

Simon
I'm sending you all the info you need for last quarter in the attachment.

I've already contacted my team and they have just finished their sales figures. Unfortunately we haven't completed the report yet as we've been very busy with trade fair prep.

The deadline should be no problem though: you'll have it on your desk by 4 May.

Rgds
Pascal

UNIT **4** Requesting action | **27**

>  **Talking about deadlines and taking action**
>
> The present perfect is used to talk about deadlines and whether or not they have been met. It is also used to describe the status of tasks in progress.
>
> ***Have** you **coordinated** your team & their results yet?*
> *I've already **contacted** my team and they **have** just **finished** their sales figures.*
>
> Adverbs like *yet*, *already*, or *just* are often used with the present perfect in this type of sentence.
>
> *Have you sent in your registration for the conference **yet**?*
> *Sorry, I haven't written the report **yet**.*
> *I've **already** sent the registration form.*
> *We've **just** received the order.*
>
> In American English the simple past is used instead of the present perfect with the signal words above. There is no difference in meaning.
>
> *Did you send in your registration **yet**?*
>
> The *will* future is used in replies to emails requesting action to say what the writer will do and when. Note that the contracted form ('*ll* instead of *will*) is usually used.
>
> *You'll **have** it on your desk by 4 May.*
> *Sorry, but I haven't sent it yet. I'**ll do** it straight away.*

2 **A virus has infected Simon's computer and scrambled Barbara's and Thilo's replies to Simon's email. Unscramble the sentences and put them in the correct order. (*Tip*: the words in bold stay where they are.)**

Barbara's reply:
a **Things** so here been busy have **that** hasn't on it there work been time to.
b **Last** desk a.m. figures will tomorrow your on quarter's be.
c **Tuesday** though be problem should no.
d **Sorry, Simon,** report yet finished I the haven't but.

Thilo's reply:
e **I've also** that the figures wanted you attached.
f **I've** the post copy put a already in **but** an too sending as attachment am it.
g **Simon, Anna** just the at account details has the sent Hungarian office.

UNIT 4 Requesting action

3 Use the words in brackets to complete the gaps in these emails.

Hello Jane

First of all, there _____ ¹ (be) a meeting next Thursday from 2 to 5 pm to discuss trade fair planning. Please let me know whether you can attend.

_____ the brochures for model 564Z and 566T _____ ² (you/order/yet)? Remember, we need 5000 copies each for the trade fair.

_____ Margot about the schedule _____ ³ (you/contact/yet)? I need the finalized version for the meeting on Thursday.

Finally, _____ the presentation material _____ ⁴ (you/send/yet)? I can't seem to find it anywhere.

Ramon

Hi Ramon

Yes, I can attend the meeting next Thursday.

I _____ ⁵ (just/order) the brochures for both models. They _____ _____ ⁶ (be delivered) on 7 September. BTW, I _____ ⁷ (just/have a look) at a pdf of the new brochure. It looks good. _____ ⁸ (you/see) it? If not, I _____ ⁹ (forward) it to you.

Re the schedule: I _____ ¹⁰ (leave) a message on Margot's voicemail but she _____ ¹¹ (call back/yet). I _____ ¹² (try) again later and _____ ¹³ (ask) her to contact you directly.

I _____ ¹⁴ (email) the presentation material straight away. Sorry for the delay.

ATB
Jane

4 Use words from the two lists to make as many verb–noun phrases as you can.

Example: *to arrange an appointment or a meeting*

arrange • attach • clarify • demand • finalize • inform • meet • notify • schedule • send • update • write

an appointment • colleagues • a database • a deadline • details • a document • a meeting • the minutes • payment • a report

UNIT 4 Requesting action 29

Now complete the sentences with words from the boxes.

1 I'm _____ you the report by post. Can you please read it and give me your feedback?
2 Please _____ your colleagues that our monthly meeting has been changed to Wednesday.
3 I've _____ an appointment with the new sales rep.
4 Clara, I've read your notes but can we meet to _____ the details.
5 I'm afraid we won't be able to meet the _____ . We're going to need a few more weeks.
6 Please email me your notes from the last meeting so that John can _____ the minutes.
7 I also need your January figures so that we can _____ the database.
8 Motor Supply Ltd still hasn't paid. It's time to demand _____ with an official letter.

5 Look at this informal reply to an email. What questions or requests did Annika write in the original email?

To: Annika Forrester <akm@jbf.com>
From: Martin Ho <mho@jbf.com>
Subject: re Internet guidelines
Attachment: internetguidelines.doc; internetaccess.xcl

Hi Annika

How are you? Thanks for your mail.

1 *Could you send me a copy of the new Internet guidelines, please?*

Yes, you can have a copy of the new Internet guidelines.
I haven't sent them yet as they only arrived this morning!
You'll find a copy attached.

2

You also asked for my thoughts about the guidelines –
no comment! :-I

3

I've also attached the stats showing Internet use in the
company – just as you asked.

4

I haven't heard from Sanji for ages either but I think she's
been on holiday. Perhaps Ian knows.

You asked if I have the dates of the next internal policies meeting
– yes, but I'll have to find them first! ;-) Will send them asap!

Look forward to your next mail.
Have a good weekend!

5

Martin

Now write the original request in full.

UNIT 4 Requesting action

6 Your boss has given you this 'to do' list before leaving on a business trip. You've ticked (✓) the jobs which have been done and added some notes. Use the 'to do' list to answer your boss's email.

- phone suppliers about our credit period ✓
  extension of 30 days
  not available on days we need!
- book room at ~~Hilton~~ for Japanese guests – want to hold reception, 10 participants approx
  booked room at International
  International
- get an offer for buffet lunch from ~~Hilton~~ ✓ *EUR 50 a person*
- check my parking permit has been renewed *can leave till end of week*
- organize times for in-company language training – NOT in core-time! ✓
- correct my overheads for Thursday presentation
- phone Jeff – cancel golf morning for Friday *left message on mailbox, will try again*
- ask Tessa to call me next Tues re: travel expenses ✓

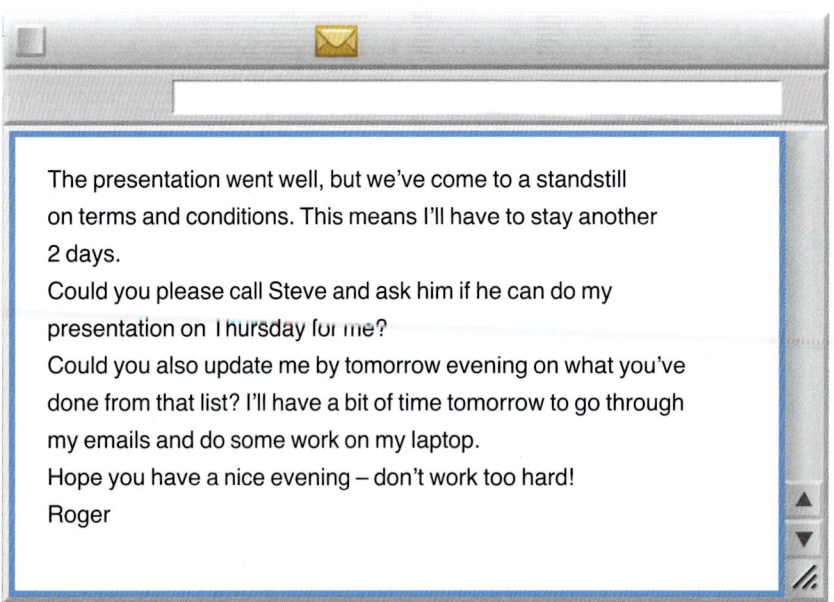

The presentation went well, but we've come to a standstill on terms and conditions. This means I'll have to stay another 2 days.
Could you please call Steve and ask him if he can do my presentation on Thursday for me?
Could you also update me by tomorrow evening on what you've done from that list? I'll have a bit of time tomorrow to go through my emails and do some work on my laptop.
Hope you have a nice evening – don't work too hard!
Roger

UNIT 4 Requesting action | 31

OUTPUT

To cc or not to cc?
Listen to five people talking about this and answer the questions below.

1. How many emails a day does she get?
2. What do they have in common?

3. What is his main point?
4. Is he happy to receive a lot of email?

5. What would she like her colleagues to do?
6. What does she mean by 'leave me out of the loop'?

7. What does his boss want?
8. What effect does this have on his working day?

9. What is his complaint?
10. What would he like to see?

OVER TO YOU

How often do you use the cc function and who do you send copies to?
Do you ever use the blind copy (bcc) function?
Does your company – or team – have a policy on who is copied in?

YOU'VE GOT MAIL ▶ UNIT 4 Partner A page 49
                              Partner B page 50

5 Exchanging information

STARTER How has email affected our business lives and relationships? Do this quiz and check your answers below. Then discuss the answers with a colleague.

1 What percentage of Internet users in the USA have email access at work?
   a. 26%
   b. 46%
   c. 66%

2 What percentage of people check their personal emails at work throughout the day?
   a. 27%
   b. 37%
   c. 47%

3 And what percentage of users said they checked emails during a business meeting?
   a. 3%
   b. 5%
   c. 8%

4 What is the most popular day of the week to send email messages?
   a. Monday
   b. Tuesday
   c. Friday

5 The majority of the online population have English as their first language (35.8%). Which languages come next?
   a. Chinese
   b. Spanish
   c. French

6 In a survey of people over 55 in the UK, what percentage said they used a computer?
   a. 36%
   b. 46%
   c. 56%

7 In a survey of UK directors and managers, what percentage said they sent more than 30 emails a day?
   a. 10%
   b. 15%
   c. 25%

8 What percentage of US workers said they have sent jokes or chain emails at work?
   a. 39%
   b. 49%
   c. 59%

1c 88% of adult Internet users in the US have a personal email account. Source: emailLabs.com (2003).

2c 25% check them first thing when they arrive at work and only 2% just before they leave for home. (See above source.)

3c The most popular place to check emails outside work was 'in bed', (23%) followed by 'in class' (12%). (See above source.)

4b About a quarter of emails are sent on Tuesday, Saturday is the least popular day, averaging at less than 1%. (See above source.)

5a Chinese makes up 14.1%, Spanish 9%, and French only 3.8%. Source: global-reach.biz (2004)

6a Of these, 82% used the computer mainly for emailing (with higher figures for women than men). These are 2002 figures, so the current total is likely to be higher. Source: icmresearch.co.uk

7c A further 40% sent between 11 and 30. Source: Ipsos-MORI.com (2001)

8a In the same survey, 15% admitted to gossiping about work on email. Source: pewinternet.org

UNIT **5** Exchanging information | **33**

1 David and Mike both work for a distribution company dealing in mobile phones. Look at David's email and answer the questions.

1 How does Mike introduce the subject of the email?
2 Label parts of the email with the following: salutation, informing, stating the action to be taken, giving a deadline, close.
3 Does David already know about the invoice? How do you know?
4 What is the new information Mike has found out?
5 What does Mike ask David to do?

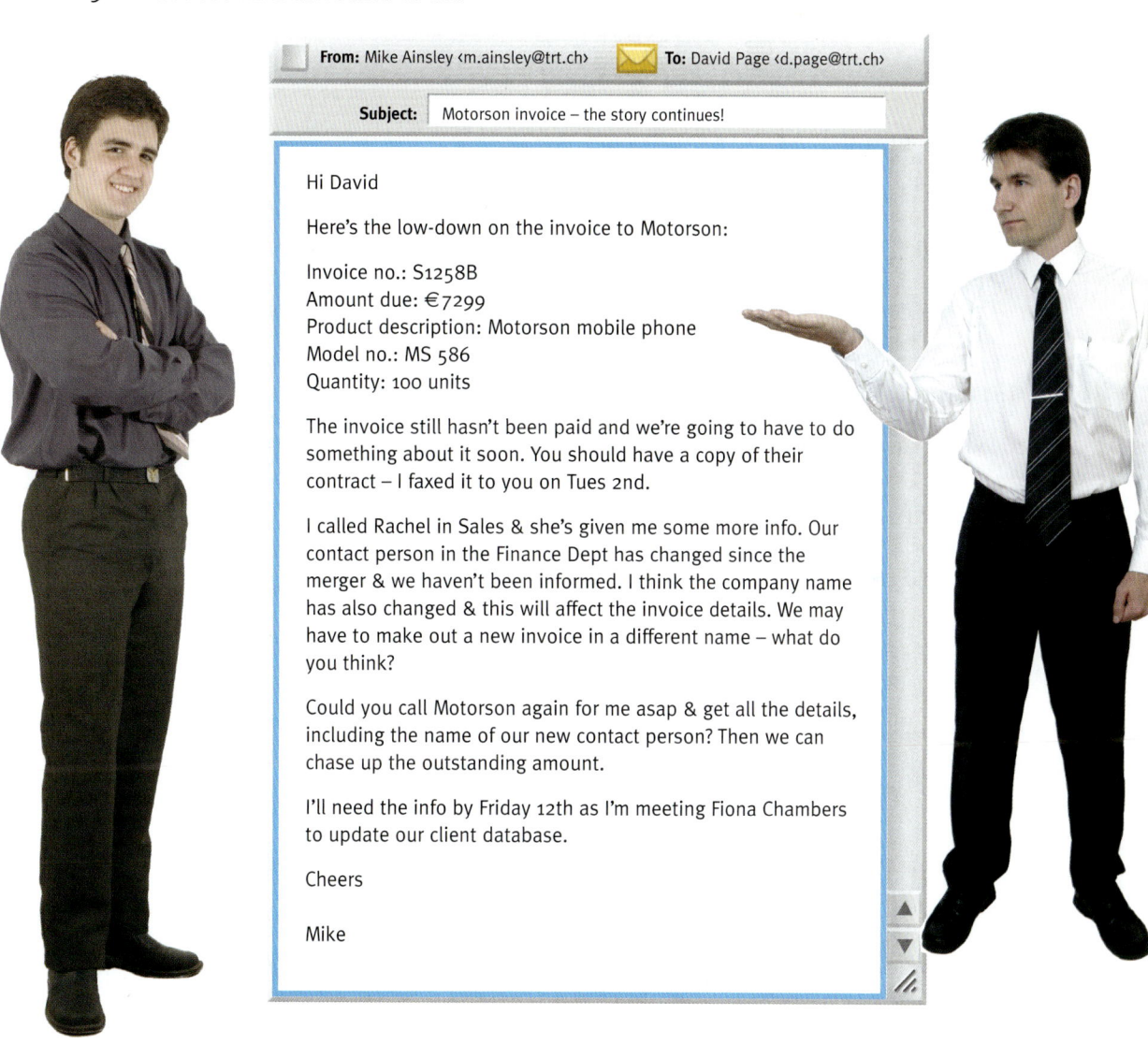

From: Mike Ainsley <m.ainsley@trt.ch> **To:** David Page <d.page@trt.ch>

Subject: Motorson invoice – the story continues!

Hi David

Here's the low-down on the invoice to Motorson:

Invoice no.: S1258B
Amount due: €7299
Product description: Motorson mobile phone
Model no.: MS 586
Quantity: 100 units

The invoice still hasn't been paid and we're going to have to do something about it soon. You should have a copy of their contract – I faxed it to you on Tues 2nd.

I called Rachel in Sales & she's given me some more info. Our contact person in the Finance Dept has changed since the merger & we haven't been informed. I think the company name has also changed & this will affect the invoice details. We may have to make out a new invoice in a different name – what do you think?

Could you call Motorson again for me asap & get all the details, including the name of our new contact person? Then we can chase up the outstanding amount.

I'll need the info by Friday 12th as I'm meeting Fiona Chambers to update our client database.

Cheers

Mike

UNIT 5 Exchanging information

 **TIP** **Colloquial phrases and contractions**

Colloquial phrases
When English native speakers write to each other as close business acquaintances they often use colloquial phrases like *the low-down*, *to chase something up* (AmE *down*), or *cheers* (BrE for *thanks*). Be careful when using colloquial phrases as they can make your English sound too familiar when used in the wrong context.

Contractions
Emails often reflect spoken English and tend to use contractions instead of the full form, e.g. *here's* (*here is*), *haven't* (*have not*), or *I'll* (*I will*).

Watch out: don't leave out the apostrophe when using contractions as the meaning could be changed.

it's = *it is*   its = *possessive*   I'll = *I will*   ill = *sick*

2 Find the matching pairs.

colloquial language	standard language
1 to check sth out	to send sb an email
2 to touch base with sb	to give sb information
3 to send sth by snail mail	to send sth by post
4 to mail* sb	to try to find or get sth (that is missing)
5 to give sb the low-down	to look at sth in detail
6 to chase sth up (AmE: *down*)	to get in contact with sb
7 to be out of the loop	to postpone sth (or put sth off)
8 to put sth on hold	to be out of touch or not have heard sth

* Watch out when *mail* is used as a verb; in AmE *to mail* also means sending something by the traditional postal service (i.e. *by snail mail*)!

Now rewrite this email using standard language to replace the colloquial phrases.

Hello Sally
Thanks for getting in touch and giving me the low-down on the March sales meeting. By the way, I called Barbara's office and tried to chase up the January figures but she's been on holiday – so no success there! Perhaps you could touch base with Gary and ask him to mail me the info directly. I hope he can – I'd hate to have to put the meeting on hold.
Oh, one last thing: can you send me a few of the new brochures? No hurry – snail mail will do!
Ciao
Jon

3 A virus has knocked out all the apostrophes in these sentences. Put them back in.

1. The employees were asked to comment on a no-smoking policy. Well report the results in our next online bulletin.
2. Were happy the negotiations ended positively for both parties.
3. Lets introduce Internet access for all of our employees. Theyve been using it for years anyway.
4. The production plants just had its yearly safety examination and no problems have been reported.
5. If you havent received the report, let me know & Ill send it on.
6. Heres the survey. Remember, well have to scrap the product if its not popular.

4 David has replied to Mike's email in exercise 1 by 'quoting' from the original message. Complete David's email with items a–e.

a No problem. According to their message, they're back on the 9th. I'll get back to you with the info asap.
b Thanks for yr email. I've written my answers in below.
c I agree. Let's discuss it with the new contact person though.
d Yes, I got it. Thanks.
e I've tried to call but the answerphone picks up. Apparently they're all on holiday! ;-) I'll keep trying though.

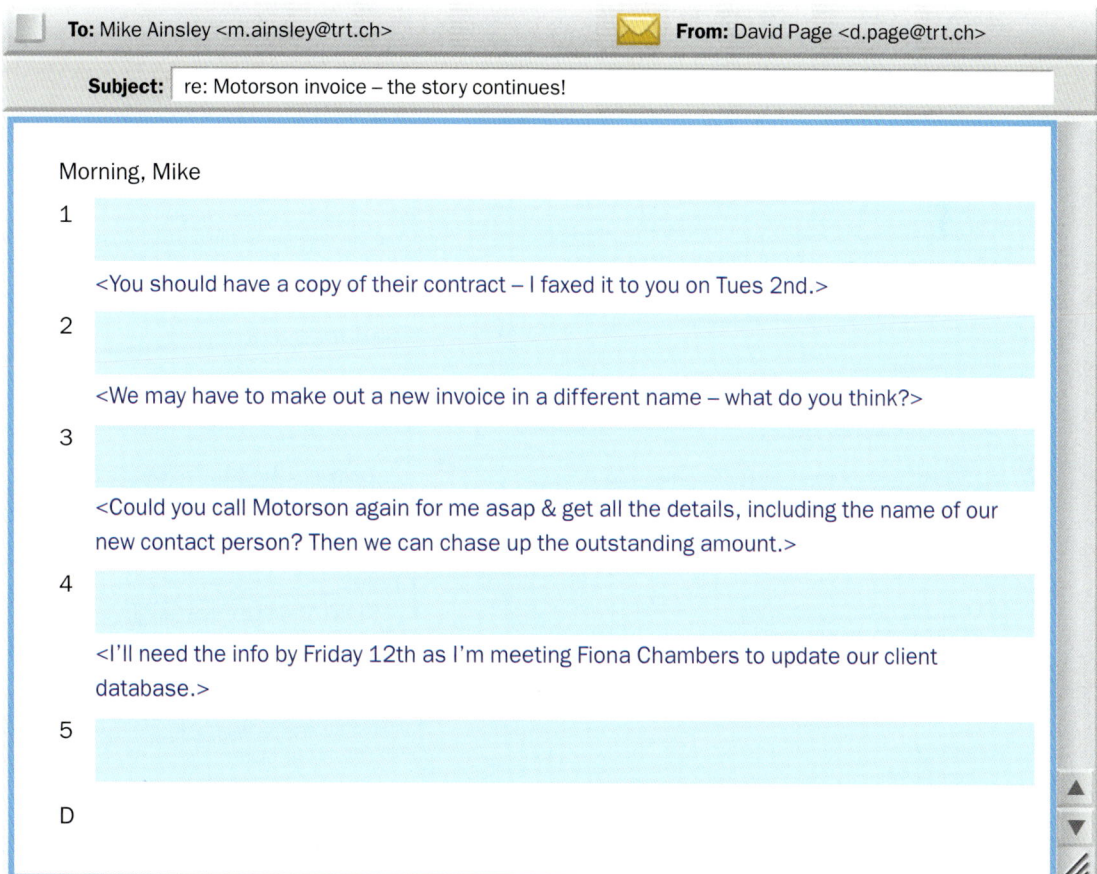

5 Put the following phrases in the correct category, informing or replying.

> Just a note to say/tell you … • In reply to your email … • Here are the details on … • I'm writing to clarify … • I'll get back to you asap … • Thank you for clarifying … • I'll follow up the points mentioned in your email … • I'd like to inform you of … • Just a few comments about/on … • Just to update you on … • Let me fill you in on … • Thanks for your email. • You'll find the info attached …

Informing

Just a note to say/tell you …

_____

_____

_____

_____

_____

Replying

In reply to your email …

_____

_____

_____

_____

_____

6 Use (parts of) the phrases in exercise 5 to complete these short emails. More than one answer may be possible.

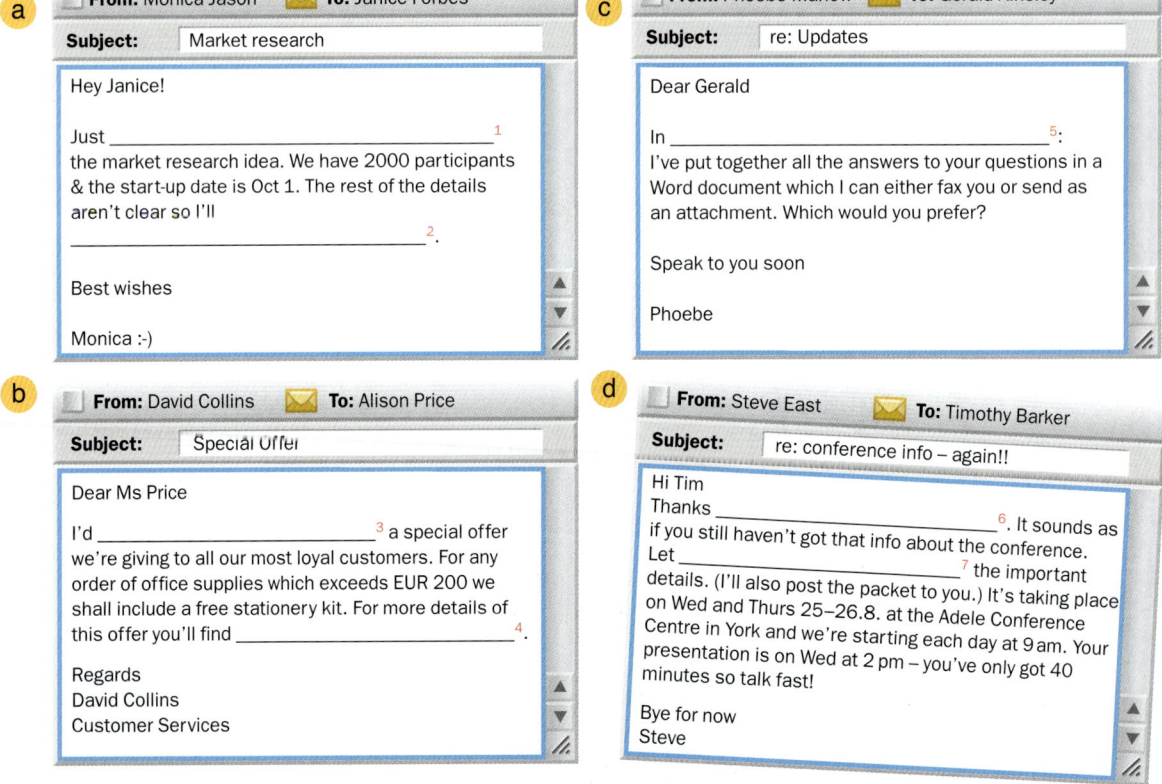

a)
From: Monica Jason To: Janice Forbes
Subject: Market research

Hey Janice!

Just _____ ¹ the market research idea. We have 2000 participants & the start-up date is Oct 1. The rest of the details aren't clear so I'll _____ ².

Best wishes

Monica :-)

b)
From: David Collins To: Alison Price
Subject: Special Offer

Dear Ms Price

I'd _____ ³ a special offer we're giving to all our most loyal customers. For any order of office supplies which exceeds EUR 200 we shall include a free stationery kit. For more details of this offer you'll find _____ ⁴.

Regards
David Collins
Customer Services

c)
From: Phoebe Marlow To: Gerald Ainsley
Subject: re: Updates

Dear Gerald

In _____ ⁵:
I've put together all the answers to your questions in a Word document which I can either fax you or send as an attachment. Which would you prefer?

Speak to you soon

Phoebe

d)
From: Steve East To: Timothy Barker
Subject: re: conference info – again!!

Hi Tim
Thanks _____ ⁶. It sounds as if you still haven't got that info about the conference. Let _____ ⁷ the important details. (I'll also post the packet to you.) It's taking place on Wed and Thurs 25–26.8. at the Adele Conference Centre in York and we're starting each day at 9 am. Your presentation is on Wed at 2 pm – you've only got 40 minutes so talk fast!

Bye for now
Steve

TIP Being diplomatic

When things aren't going according to plan, an email exchange can become heated. The use of diplomatic language lets you point out mistakes gently, without offending the person you're writing to.

> We have a **slight / minor / little** problem.
> **Unfortunately**, the mistake is **rather** serious.
> **I'm afraid** we're not happy with …

Furthermore, be careful when showing emotion in an email. Using exclamation marks and writing words or phrases in capital letters can make your message too strong – it can look like you're shouting.

> Joanne, I'm still waiting for a reply!!!
> Didn't we agree to meet on TUESDAY?

A more moderate way to emphasize a word is to enclose it in asterisks.

> Just writing to see what happened to your report. I needed it *Monday* and it's now Friday. Can we discuss?

7 Rewrite the following email to make it more diplomatic.

Bob
We have a problem! I asked you to send me the conference details LAST WEEK but I still haven't received anything. What's going on?!! Now the hotel has asked me for the info today or we will lose the reservation. This is NOT a good situation!!! This is the ONLY hotel available in Madstown for our dates and I don't want to have to change the conference location.
PLEASE TAKE CARE OF THIS IMMEDIATELY!
Jack

UNIT 5 Exchanging information

8 Use these notes to write emails to some colleagues.

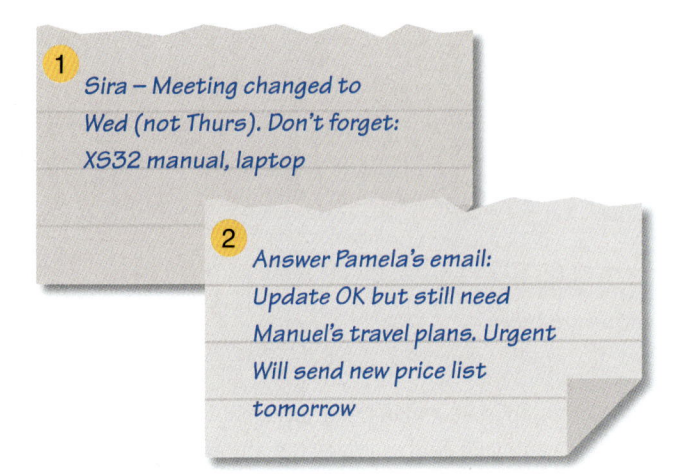

1. Sira – Meeting changed to Wed (not Thurs). Don't forget: XS32 manual, laptop

2. Answer Pamela's email:
Update OK but still need Manuel's travel plans. Urgent
Will send new price list tomorrow

3. Email John with update (check with Alice to make sure he's back from holiday) YES!
Still no answer from Izumi about the Appleton account.
Gantor-Brooks acct has been approved
Meeting with me, Paul, and Izumi next week (Thursday 9 am) if he has time?

OUTPUT

Cecil Armstrong is a trainer for office communication. In this interview he talks about one of his 'pet hates' – something which annoys him when he is using email as a communication tool.

AUDIO 7

Listen to the interview and answer the questions below.

1. What does Cecil really dislike?
2. Why?
3. What does he recommend?
4. What's his number one rule for email etiquette?

The email printout? Should take ... ooh, only about, ahem, an hour ...

OVER TO YOU

What do you think about quoting in emails? Do you ever do it?
Does it bother you as much as it does Cecil?
Is there anything which really annoys you when you receive emails? Write a list of 'five things NOT to do'.

YOU'VE GOT MAIL ▶ UNIT 5   Partner A page 49
Partner B page 51

6 Making and confirming arrangements

STARTER

The domain name is the part of the email address which comes after the 'at' sign (@).
Find the part of the domain for someone who ...

.ac.uk • .at • .au • .ca • .ch • .co.uk • .com • .net • .es • .gov • ibm.de • .org

1 works for a company which is probably in the US.
2 works for a German division of a computer hardware company.
3 is writing from Australia.
4 is writing from Austria.
5 works for a non-profit organization.
6 works for a British university.
7 works for an Internet service provider.
8 lives in Switzerland.
9 is writing from Canada.
10 works for the US government.
11 is writing from Spain.
12 works for a company in England.

Now match the country codes to the countries (1–20).

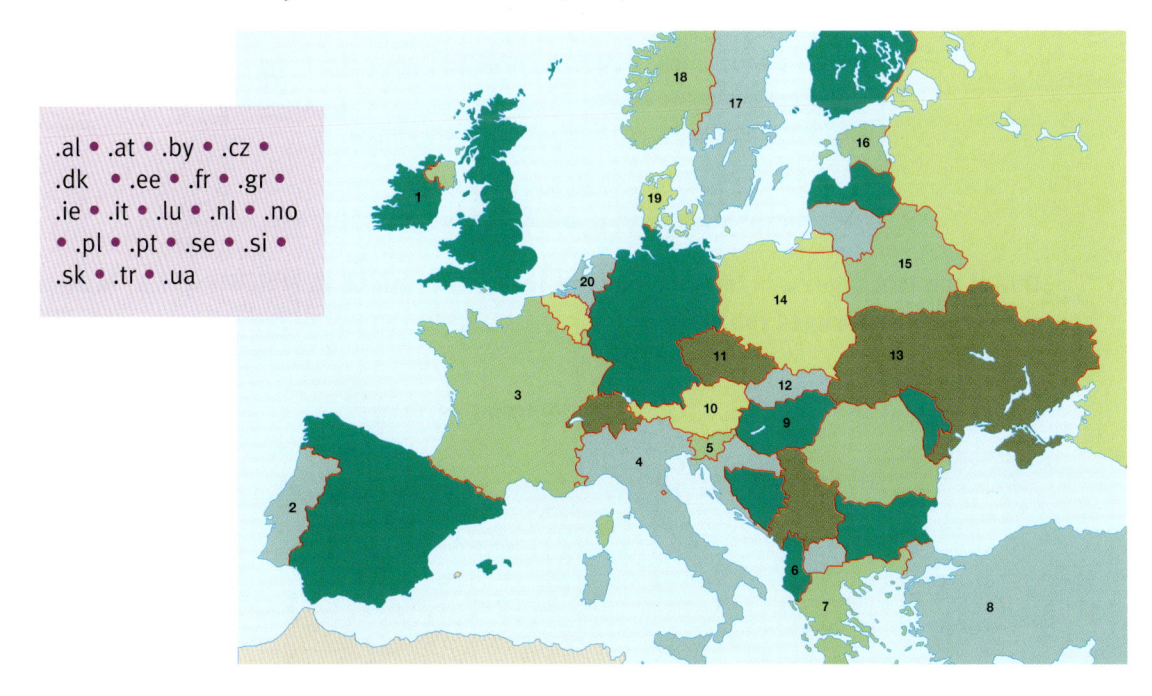

.al • .at • .by • .cz • .dk • .ee • .fr • .gr • .ie • .it • .lu • .nl • .no • .pl • .pt • .se • .si • .sk • .tr • .ua

UNIT 6 Making and confirming arrangements

1 Below are two email exchanges. Match the emails with their replies.

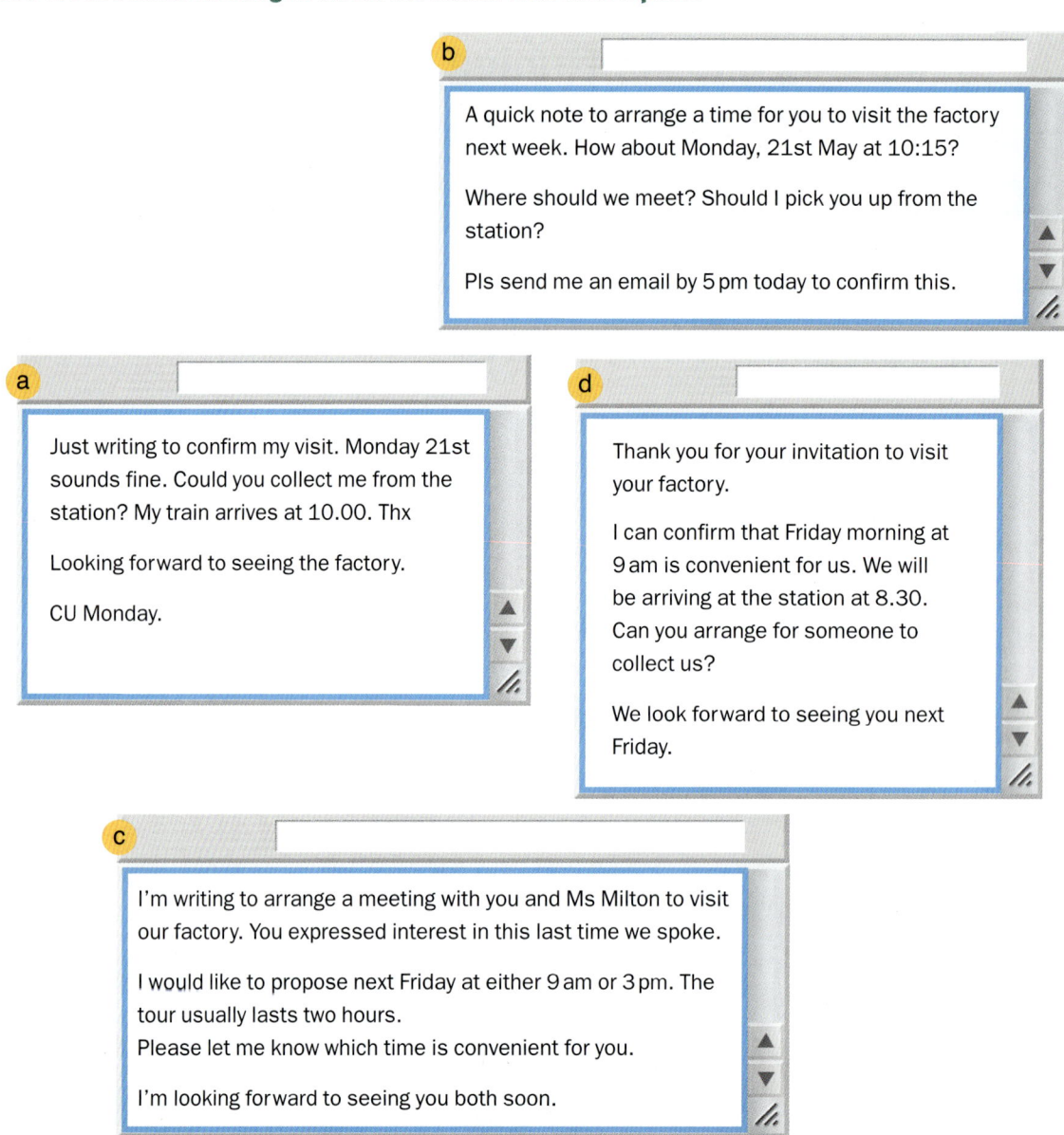

b
A quick note to arrange a time for you to visit the factory next week. How about Monday, 21st May at 10:15?

Where should we meet? Should I pick you up from the station?

Pls send me an email by 5 pm today to confirm this.

a
Just writing to confirm my visit. Monday 21st sounds fine. Could you collect me from the station? My train arrives at 10.00. Thx

Looking forward to seeing the factory.

CU Monday.

d
Thank you for your invitation to visit your factory.

I can confirm that Friday morning at 9 am is convenient for us. We will be arriving at the station at 8.30. Can you arrange for someone to collect us?

We look forward to seeing you next Friday.

c
I'm writing to arrange a meeting with you and Ms Milton to visit our factory. You expressed interest in this last time we spoke.

I would like to propose next Friday at either 9 am or 3 pm. The tour usually lasts two hours.
Please let me know which time is convenient for you.

I'm looking forward to seeing you both soon.

One of the exchanges is in formal language, the other is informal. Which is which? Make a list of the phrases that helped you decide.

formal

informal

2 Find phrases in the emails in exercise 1 to complete the gaps.

Making arrangements

Organizing a date and a time

I'm writing to ar_____¹.

A quick note to ar_____² to meet.

Just writing to organize a time for your visit.
When would suit you best?
What about 5 o'clock?

H_____³ Tuesday?

Is 5 o'clock suitable?
Is Tuesday convenient?
Is 3 p.m. OK?

Please let me know wh_____⁴.

Please let me know if this is convenient.

Organizing a meeting place

Where should w_____⁵?

Should I p_____⁶ from the station?

Should I collect you from the airport?

Could you c_____⁷?

Could you arrange for s_____⁸?

Meet me at the station.
I'll see you at reception.

Confirming arrangements

I'd like to confirm my visit.

Just writing to c_____⁹ the arrangements.

I can confirm that 9 a.m. is c_____¹⁰.

I'd prefer Friday at 8 a.m.
5 o'clock is good for me/is fine.
Tuesday sounds great/suits me.
Let me know if this is OK.

Please send me an email by 5 p.m. today to c_____¹¹.

I look forward to meeting you.

L_____¹² seeing the factory.

See you on Tuesday!

3 Use the phrases below to complete the two emails.

> good for me • I look forward to • Is 12.30 OK • send me an email • to confirm • what about • writing to arrange

From: Vanessa <v.peters@tedelex.at> **To:** Sandra <sandra-schuetz@web1.at>
Subject: Meeting to discuss presentation

Dear Sandra

Just _____ [1] a meeting to discuss the presentation. _____ [2] Friday? We could meet for lunch at the Trattoria Rialto on Breite Strasse. _____ [3]?

Pls _____ [4] this afternoon to confirm.

Regards
Vanessa

From: Sandra <sandra-schuetz@web1.at> **To:** Vanessa <v.peters@tedelex.at>
Subject: re: Meeting to discuss presentation

Dear Vanessa

I'd like _____ [5] our meeting on Friday.

12:30 is _____ [6]. I'll bring the presentation info with me.

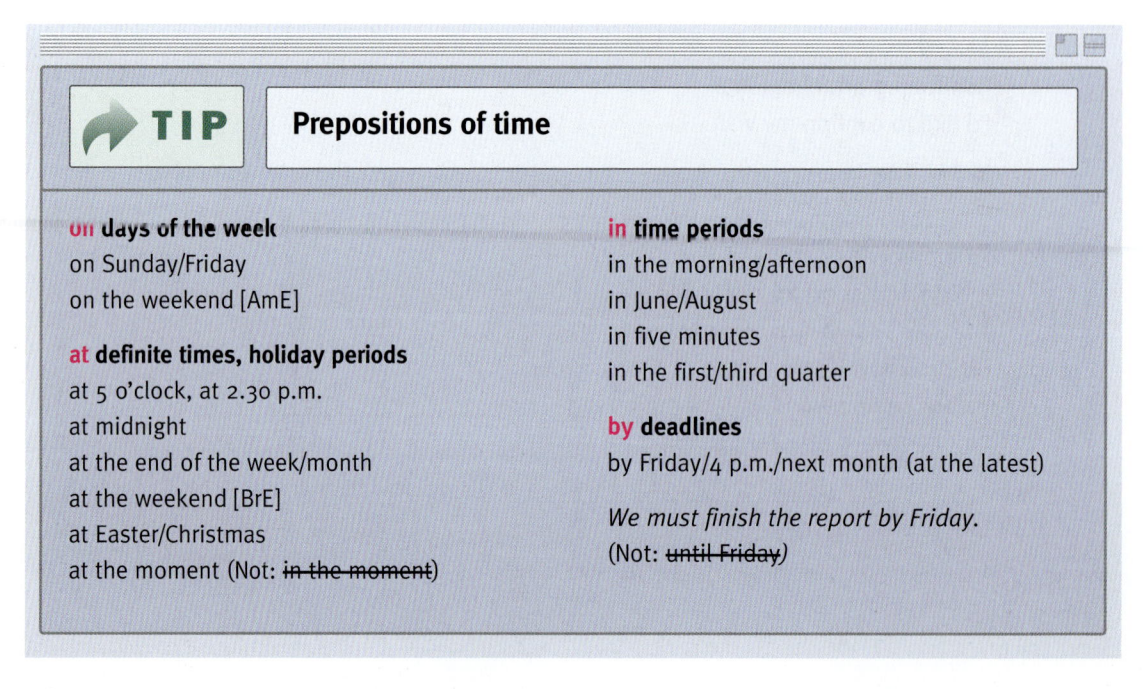

_____ [7] seeing you on Friday.

Sandra

BTW – rgds to Jim!

TIP — Prepositions of time

on days of the week
on Sunday/Friday
on the weekend [AmE]

at definite times, holiday periods
at 5 o'clock, at 2.30 p.m.
at midnight
at the end of the week/month
at the weekend [BrE]
at Easter/Christmas
at the moment (Not: ~~in the moment~~)

in time periods
in the morning/afternoon
in June/August
in five minutes
in the first/third quarter

by deadlines
by Friday/4 p.m./next month (at the latest)

We must finish the report by Friday.
(Not: ~~until Friday~~)

UNIT 6 Making and confirming arrangements | 43

4 Read the following sentences and cross out the incorrect prepositions.

1 The conference begins ~~at~~ / on / ~~in~~ Monday at / on / in the afternoon.
2 Could you pick me up at / with / on 5 o'clock?
3 The report must be finished in / by / at Tuesday.
4 All holidays must be taken at / on / in June.
5 The company was founded by / in / on 2001.
6 I'll be at a client's in / at / on the end of the week.
7 On / In / At the moment I'm very busy but I'll be able to finish the report by / until / on next week.
8 If I haven't heard from you by / in / at the weekend, I'll call you in / on / at Saturday.

5 Use the notes below to write an email to a client to set up a meeting.

> Tues
> second meeting to finalize terms and conditions next week
> three possible times:
> Monday 13/3 2 pm
> Thursday 16/3, any time
> Friday 17/3 morning any time
> need approx 2 hours
> (Urgent: deadline for reserving conference room tomorrow noon!)

6 Now look at the client's diary and write a response.

MONDAY BA 3452 Edinburgh conference (meeting with JT 15.00)
TUESDAY Presentation 10–11.30
         Return flight 16.10
WEDNESDAY
THURSDAY 9.00–12.00 Meeting J. Thomas
          Pick up TG at airport 17.00
FRIDAY Assessment Centre 9.00–15.00
SATURDAY
SUNDAY

UNIT 6 Making and confirming arrangements

7 **Nigel Sharp receives the following reply to an email he sent. What words or expressions does Christine use to:**

1 say that the suggested dates are not convenient? Find two examples.
2 say that she's sorry? Find two examples.
3 suggest changing the meeting to a later date?
4 suggest a new time to meet?

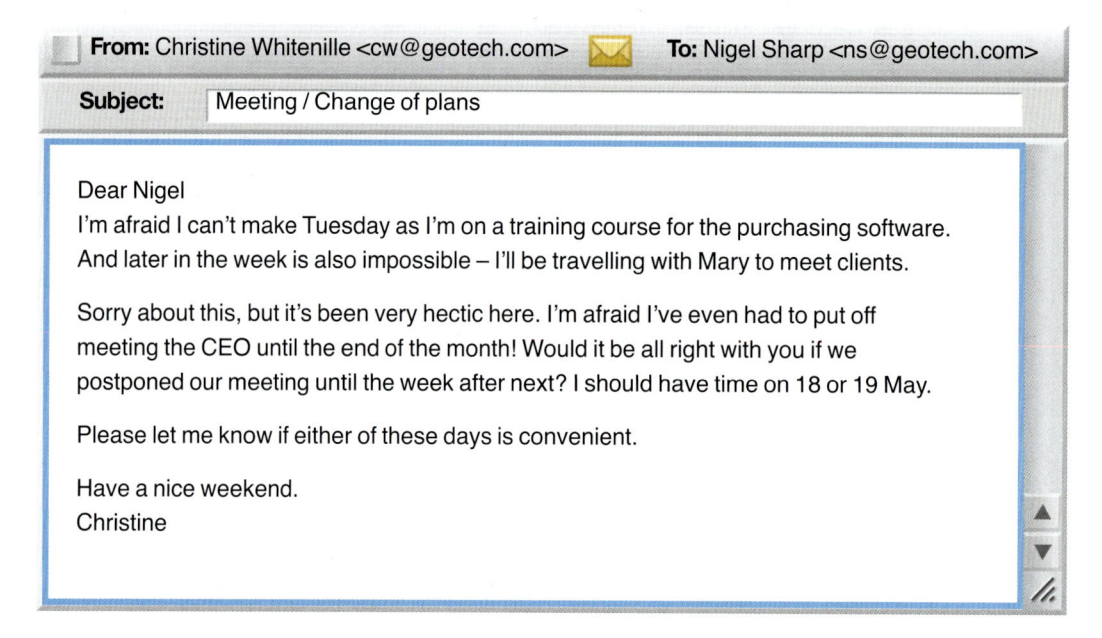

From: Christine Whitenille <cw@geotech.com>   **To:** Nigel Sharp <ns@geotech.com>
Subject: Meeting / Change of plans

Dear Nigel
I'm afraid I can't make Tuesday as I'm on a training course for the purchasing software. And later in the week is also impossible – I'll be travelling with Mary to meet clients.

Sorry about this, but it's been very hectic here. I'm afraid I've even had to put off meeting the CEO until the end of the month! Would it be all right with you if we postponed our meeting until the week after next? I should have time on 18 or 19 May.

Please let me know if either of these days is convenient.

Have a nice weekend.
Christine

---

8 **You receive the following email but the time and dates don't work out for you. Use the words below to write a reply.**

I'm afraid • postpone • by Monday • would it be all right • can't make it

---

Dear Marion
Just writing to arrange a meeting to discuss the schedule for the new project. Unfortunately, next week looks quite busy but I do have time on Tuesday, 25 January. *No time Tuesday. Wednesday or Friday at 9.00*
I'd prefer an early morning meeting (perhaps at 8 am) and would suggest we meet at the Coffee Pot Café so we can have a ('working breakfast'). *Don't like breakfast meetings. My office?*
Is this convenient for you?
Could you get back to me by 6 pm today as I'm out of the office for the rest of the week?
Cheers
Jason
Answer needed Monday latest (I'm away Tuesday)

UNIT 6 Making and confirming arrangements 45

OUTPUT

Listen to this report on spam and answer the questions below.

AUDIO 8

> **spam** /spæm/ N (IT informal) Advertising material sent by email to large numbers of people who have not asked for it.

1. What examples of spam does the presenter mention?
2. Who is sending it and from where?
3. What is the best way to stop getting spam?
4. Are filters efficient?
5. What figures does Alex quote?
6. What is the legal situation?
7. What advice does Alex offer?
8. What forecast does he make?

Over to you

Do you receive spams? If so, what do you do with them?
How can companies stop junk mail from entering their systems?
Do you think there should be stricter regulations regarding junk mail?

YOU'VE GOT MAIL ▶ UNIT 6   Partner A page 49
Partner B page 51

Test yourself!

See how much you've learned about writing emails in English.
Use the clues to complete the crossword puzzle.

Across

2. A word meaning 'the latest date to finish something, like a report'.
5. *to make clear*: *I'm writing to … the terms of the agreement.*
7. An abbreviated expression for *as fast as you can*.
10. electronic junk mail
12. To give somebody the most recent information: *Just writing to … you on the changes.*
13. You do this when you send an email you've received to a third person.
15. *to make contact*: *This is to … base before the conference.*
17. Anagram: MRINOCF (to say something is true)
20. You do this when you want to remove a message from your inbox.
21. A way to start an email: *… a quick note to say hi.*
22. Another word for *answer*. *Looking forward to your ….*
23. Another word for *happy*: *We would be … if you could send us ….*
27. Complete the phrase: *Sorry I can't … Thursday. How about Monday?*
28. The eleventh character in this email address: info@trans-com.at
29. The fifteenth character in the above address.

Down

1. An informal email salutation.
3. Another way to say *inform me* (3 words): *Please … if you need anything else.*
4. A preposition used to talk about deadlines: *I need the report … Monday.*
6. A polite way to say something unpleasant: *I'm … I haven't done the report yet.*
7. A document you send using email.
8. The missing word: *We are having a few problems … the moment.*
9. The sixth character in this email address: carol_banks@gt.ch
11. You do this to an appointment when you move it to a later date.
13. You can write this in your subject line or at the beginning of an email to show you just want to give information and don't expect a reply.
14. Another, more formal word for *help*.
16. If you delay a project or a decision, you *put it on ….*
18. Two letters used to introduce the subject of an email.
19. The full form of *pls*.
24. A standard close to a more formal email.
25. Anagram: TUNRGE (very important)
26. A way to end an email when you want a reply: *Looking forward to … from you.*

Now fill in the letters from the puzzle to find a final tip for writing a good, accurate email.

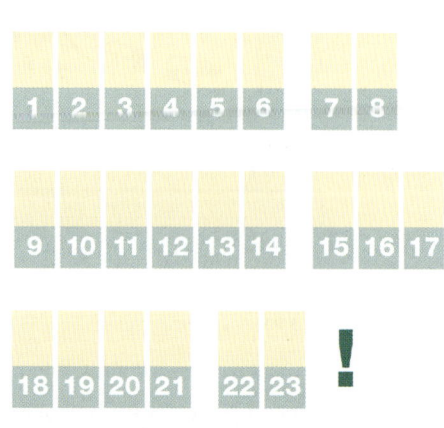

Test yourself! | 47

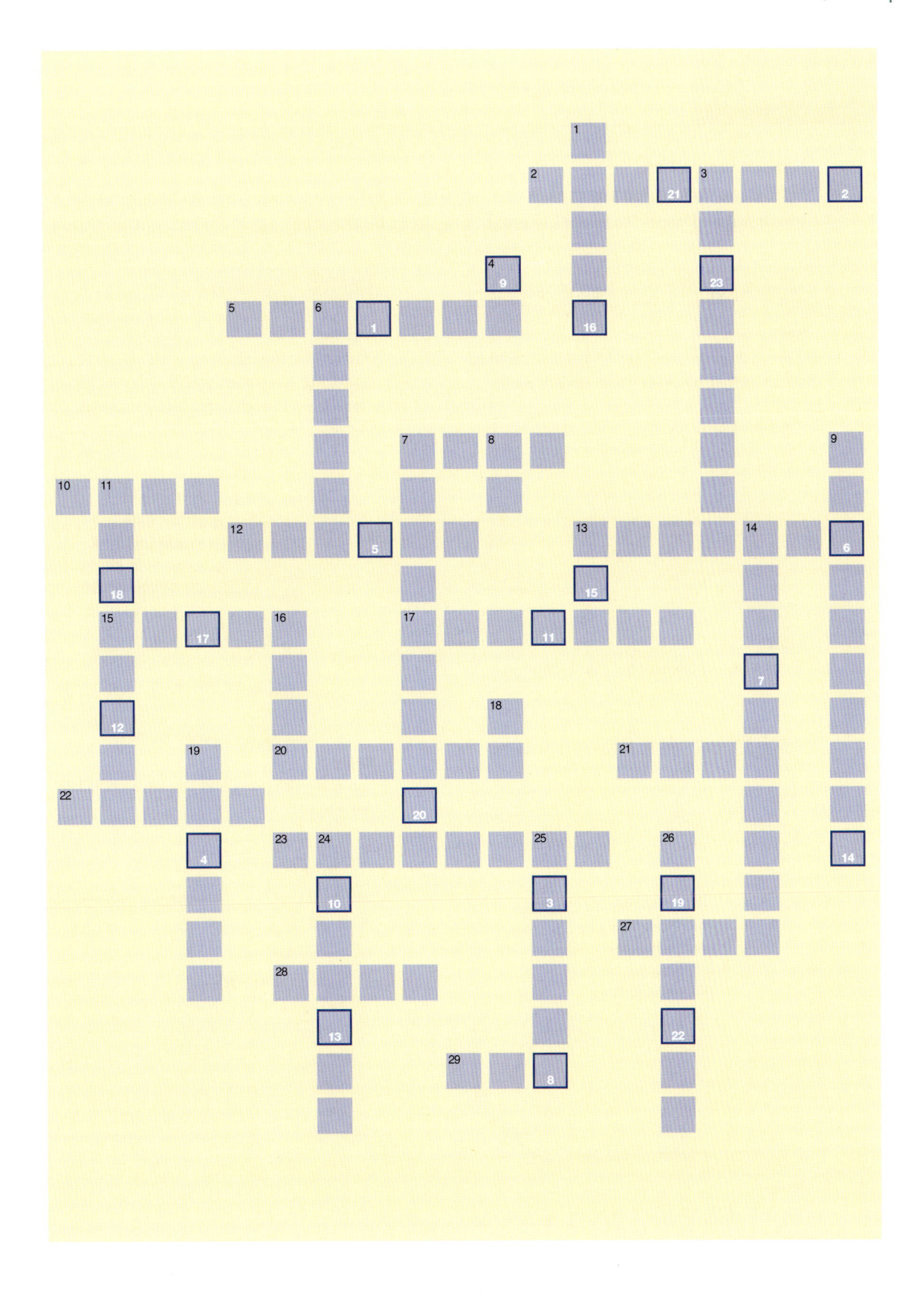

Partner A — You've got mail!

General instructions
Follow the instruction under each unit heading to 'write' an email. Then exchange emails with Partner B and 'reply' to his or her email. Check the instructions again for extra information.

Unit 1   An introduction to emails

Write
Write a short email to a colleague. Tell him/her about Steven Rosenstein's retirement party.

> *Invitation*
>
> Friday 20th August
>
> 6 pm
>
> at Joey's Bar

Reply
Thank your supplier for the information.

Unit 2   Formal & informal emails

Write
Your boss left this post-it note on your desk while you were at lunch. Follow the instructions she gave you.

> Please email Ronald Chambers (r.chambers@jsu.com). We need his company's phone number and delivery address for our customer database.
>
> Don't forget these are new clients. Be nice!
>
> Thanks, Jan

Reply
You receive an email from a former colleague. Reply to it.

Unit 3   Enquiries

Write
You receive the information below. Write an email to Brian, but remember, you've only met him once at a trade fair and exchanged business cards.

> Can you ask that guy Brian who you met at the last international trade fair if he can send us some info about their new product? It would be great if he could give us a demo too!
>
> Thanks! Kirsten

Reply
You work at a hotel and receive an email. Write a reply to it.

> *Our Facilities*
>
> 4 large meeting rooms, 1 seats 60 people, 1 seats 40 people, 2 seat 20 people
>
> Technical support
>
> Swimming pool and sauna
>
> Restaurant (weekends – restaurant only open evenings; for lunchtime arrangements our staff are happy to reserve you a table at a local restaurant)
>
> Internet access in residents' lounge

Unit 4   Requesting action

Write

Write an email to your colleague requesting action. You need:
- 2 quarterly reports (regions 1 & 2), deadlines end of week & middle of next week
- information about competitor's new product
- minutes of last meeting

Reply

You receive an email from a customer. Reply to it, using the order form and the note from your boss below.

Order form

1. 25 white radiators, style "Richmond", item no. RI 539
2. 5 glass shower cabinets, style "Estelle", item no. ES 651
3. 12 oval mirrors with light, style "Helio", item no. HE 824
4. 6 bathroom cabinets – pine, style "Rustic", item no. RU 418
5. 10 shower taps, style "Nostalgia", item no. NO 332
6. 7 towel rails – chrom, style "Moderne", item no. MO 739

> 1) already sent – arrival end of week 12th Feb approx
> 2+3) not in stock
> 4) to be sent tomorrow – 9th Feb, take 2 weeks to arrive
> 5) already sent – arrival end of week 12th Feb approx
> 6) will be sent next week – arrival approx. 3 weeks – 2nd March

Unit 5   Exchanging information

Write

Read the information on the note and put it into an email.

> Could you let Willi know about the promotion dates (5 – 15th January)? Ask him if he's got the market research results back & send him the packaging design.
>
> Cheers
> Sid

Reply

Reply to the email you have received.

Unit 6   Making and confirming arrangements

Write

You need to set up a meeting with your colleague to discuss a new promotion. The meeting will take about two hours. Write an email to your colleague to arrange this. Use the diary below to decide when you can meet.

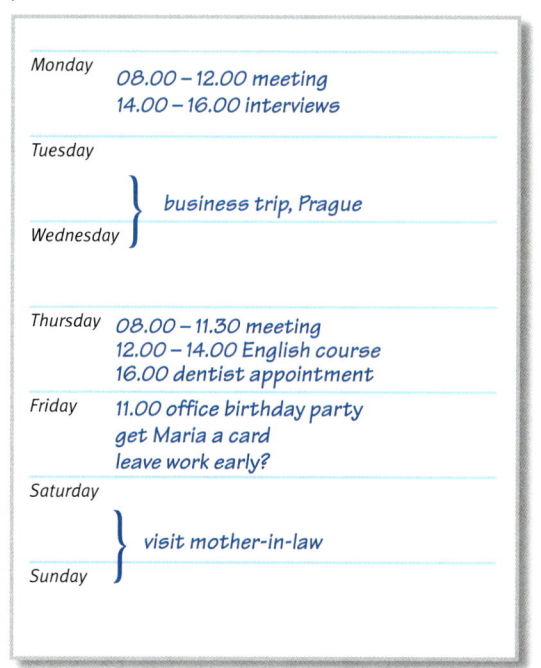

> Monday   08.00 – 12.00 meeting
>   14.00 – 16.00 interviews
>
> Tuesday   } business trip, Prague
> Wednesday }
>
> Thursday 08.00 – 11.30 meeting
>   12.00 – 14.00 English course
>   16.00 dentist appointment
>
> Friday   11.00 office birthday party
>   get Maria a card
>   leave work early?
>
> Saturday } visit mother-in-law
> Sunday   }

Reply

Reply to the email, confirming the date. The time is too early, suggest a later time and a location.

Partner B — You've got mail!

General instructions
Follow the instruction under each unit heading to 'write' an email. Then exchange emails with Partner A and 'reply' to his or her email. Check the instructions again for extra information.

Unit 1 An introduction to emails

Write
Write an email to a client. You have some new brochures, which will be in the post today. The prices have changed though!

Reply
Thank your colleague for the reminder. You're definitely going. Keep the email short.

Unit 2 Formal & informal emails

Write
You receive this memo at work.

---
memo

Dear Colleagues
We're pleased to announce that Carol has been promoted to head the Logistics Department, beginning March 1. We're sure you'll join us in congratulating her & wishing her good luck!

You worked with Carol for many years before changing departments. Send her an email.

Reply
You receive an email from your potential supplier. Reply to it using the following information.

> **To:** Purchasing Dept
> **From:** Management (Jakob Leitner)
>
> Message:
> Due to warehouse location change, our delivery address is now:
> Avenida Diagonal, 643
> 08034 Barcelona
> Spain
> Tel. no. +34 93 280 4923
> Please make sure NOTHING is sent to this address until 1st July.
> JL

Unit 3 Enquiries

Write
You are organizing a small conference and would like to receive an offer from a few hotels.
Use the information below to write an enquiry.

- Dates: Saturday & Sunday (3rd & 4th Sept)
- Participants: 45
- 10 participants need rooms
- buffet at lunchtime
- 3 meeting rooms for 15–20 people

Reply
Reply to the email you receive. You remember meeting the writer and can do what he/she asks.

Unit 4 Requesting action

Write
You have waited three weeks for an order of goods, which should have been with the forwarders last week. Send an email, asking your supplier to send you a list of what has already been sent & the expected arrival date.
Your original order is below.

> **Order form**
> – 25 white radiators, style "Richmond", item no. RI 539
> – 5 glass shower cabinets, style "Estelle", item no. ES 651
> – 12 oval mirrors with light, style "Helio", item no. HE 824
> – 6 bathroom cabinets – pine, style "Rustic", item no. RU 418
> – 10 shower taps, style "Nostalgia", item no. NO 332
> – 7 towel rails – chrome, style "Moderne", item no. MO 739

Reply

You receive an email from one of your colleagues. Look at your 'to do' list and reply to it.

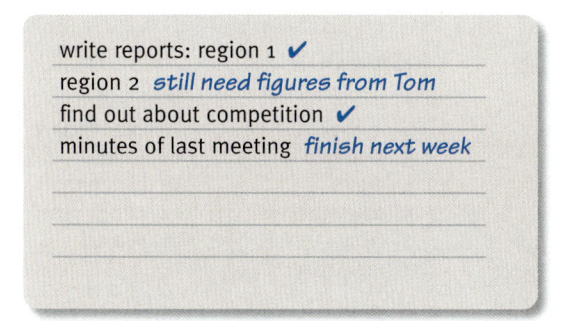

> write reports: region 1 ✔
> region 2 *still need figures from Tom*
> find out about competition ✔
> minutes of last meeting *finish next week*

Unit 5 Exchanging information

Write

Send an email to your team, informing them when you are on holiday. Tell them who will be the contact person while you're away and also ask them for their holiday dates so you can put them in the diary.

Reply

Reply to the email you have received using the summary and the note from your boss below.

Summary of Market Research Results:

Product "Minty" sweets
1. Design: can remain the same, was liked by testers
2. Strength of flavour: consumers complained, mint too hot!
3. Size: make slightly smaller, reduce amount to 25g
4. Advertising: fine! Positive feedback, especially the trial packs

> *Pls thank for packaging design attachment! Looks good!*

Unit 6 Making and confirming arrangements

Write

Write to a client, suggesting a date & time to meet (add your own details). You would like him/her to suggest the place.

Reply

You receive an email. Can you meet on the day suggested? Reply, either confirming or suggesting another date.
Use the diary below.

Monday	*trade fair*
Tuesday	*trade fair*
Wednesday	*09.00 doctor's appointment* *11.00 –13.00 lunch appointment with French visitors* *14.00 – 16.00 update meeting*
Thursday	
Friday	*08.00 – 09.00 breakfast at Hotel Metropol*
Saturday	
Sunday	*camping with the kids*

STARTER Unit 3

First write down the email and website addresses that your partner dictates.

1 _____
2 _____
3 _____
4 _____
5 _____

Then dictate these addresses to your partner:

6 http://news.bcj.co.uk
7 biz.bod@fnc.com
8 www.blc_clf.at
9 tt-dant@blackley.fr
10 HarlieJoy.xr@dante.it

Answer key

UNIT 1

page 5

Starter
(Suggested answers – open for discussion!)

1 Agree and disagree: On the one hand, emails and letters are both written forms of communication, so you need some of the same basic language skills to write them well, e.g. good organization, clear and concise language, correct grammar and appropriate vocabulary. On the other hand, emails **are** different from letters in terms of style, register, and language used, so you need some different skills as well. This book will help you develop the language skills needed to write good emails in English.

2 Agree and disagree: It is true that emails (especially informal ones) share some of the same vocabulary and style as spoken messages. But this type of informal language is not usually suitable when writing emails in a professional context. (See Unit 2 *Formal & informal emails*.)

3 Agree: Not only is the subject line useful for telling the recipient what the email is about before it is read, but it is also helpful for finding the email later when it is filed away in the inbox. (See exercise 4 on page 8.)

4 Agree: You might find native speakers do not always correct mistakes in their emails. This can be acceptable – especially in internal emails – as long as the mistakes do not interfere with communication. On the other hand, even if the message is clear, too many mistakes can give a bad impression. (See OUTPUT on page 17 for discussion.)

5 Agree and disagree: Copying others in to your email exchange does help keep everybody informed about what is happening or what decisions have been made (and might even reduce the time spent in meetings!). But the option is often overused and can waste people's time when they have to read a lot of emails every day. (See OUTPUT on page 31 for discussion.)

6 Agree: As an email is received within minutes or even seconds, the writer usually expects an immediate response, even if it is just to say that the email has arrived and will be answered later.

7 Agree and disagree: It **is** more direct to reach for the phone, but with email you have the information in writing. Furthermore, you may pick an inconvenient time when you phone somebody, whereas an email can be read and answered when the other person has time.

page 6

1
1 inbox
2 outbox
3 sent items
4 drafts
5 deleted items
6 reply
7 reply to all
8 forward
9 send/receive
10 contacts
11 high priority
12 attachment
13 subject

2
1 In 'sent items'.
2 In the inbox.
3 With the 'forward' command.
4 In 'contacts'.
5 In 'drafts'.
6 In the subject line.
7 With the 'high priority' command.
8 In the attachment.

3 Differences are: the salutation (*Hello* instead of *Dear*); the use of informal language and abbreviations (*hope* instead of *I hope* or *info* for *information*); close (*Regards* instead of *With best regards* or *Yours sincerely*); use of subject line; layout; the length (shorter and more concise than a letter); use of contracted forms (*haven't* for *have not*, *here's* for *here is*).

page 8

4
1 e
2 c
3 a
4 e
5 f
6 i
7 h
8 l
9 j or k

5 Model answers
1 REQ: new production schedule
2 re: handbook XL20 motor
3 holiday from 3–5 Oct
4 meeting: time change
5 REQ: staff guidelines
6 Confirmation of order no 66193F/2

page 9

6

	Formal email	Informal email
salutation	h	e
opening sentence	g	b
body	a	i
friendly ending	j	c
close	d	f

page 10

7
1 regards
2 outbox
3 subject
4 forward
5 receive
6 high priority
7 message
8 reply
9 inbox
10 writing

The hidden word is **attachment**.

Answer key

Output
1 They are scanning and checking their employees' emails.
2 Many employees aren't happy.
3 They're worried about inappropriate emails (e.g. jokes that could be interpreted as sexual harassment or emails that reveal company secrets).

1	productivity	5	computers
2	monitoring	6	toys
3	firms	7	receive
4	spend	8	working

UNIT 2

page 11

Starter

1	c	8	:-)
2	d	9	O:-)
3	f	10	:-O
4	g	11	:-(
5	b	12	:->
6	a	13	;-)
7	e	14	:-I

pages 12–13

1 The formal emails are: a, c, d, f.
The informal emails are: b, e.

page 13

2
1	f	3	e	5	d
2	b	4	c	6	a

page 14

3 Suggested answer

More formal	Less formal (or informal)
salutations & closes	
Dear Mr Braithwaite	Hey Gary!
Yours sincerely	Hello Gabi
Regards	See ya
Kind regards	Have a nice day
Thank you for your cooperation.	
phrases & vocabulary	
We would also appreciate …	I'm off to …
Please could you …	Just a note to tell you …
	Would it be OK if …
	Hope you …
(following can also be used in informal emails)	Speak to you …
I'm writing to …	tell (instead of *inform*)
Thank you for …	put off (a visit) (instead of *postpone*)
I would like to …	trouble (instead of *inconvenience*)
to inform	
to confirm	
to enquire	
to appreciate	

More formal	Less formal (or informal)
abbreviations, etc	
rep	info
	rep, memo (can also be used in formal emails)
	&
	:-)

page 15

4
2	help	7	to put off
3	to tell	8	to set up
4	to answer	9	to ask
5	to be sorry	10	to need
6	to get in touch with		

5
1	enquire	7	sorry
2	require	8	put off
3	arrange	9	need
4	inform	10	ask
5	convenient	11	set up
6	contact	12	get in touch

page 16

6
2	as soon as possible	7	attention
3	Thursday	8	regards
4	January	9	please
5	at the moment	10	weekend
6	Best wishes		

7 Email 1 is informal. It contains a colloquial phrase (*a bit of info*), abbreviations (*pls*), an emoticon, an informal salutation (*Hi*) and no close. Furthermore some words are omitted (*I was wondering, I'm not sure*). See page 25 for more on this topic.

Email 2 is more formal. It contains a formal open and close (*Dear, Best regards*), more formal vocabulary (*attend, assist, arrange*) and no abbreviations or emoticons. Furthermore, although contractions are used (common in all emails), no words are omitted.

Model answers
Hi Teresa
Nice to hear from you.
The Hotel Bern is very central, but a bit expensive. It's OK if your company's paying! Otherwise, you could have a look at the following website address which has a lot of good hotels & B&Bs. The address is: www.berncityscope.ch/accommodation.htm.
I'm sending you a map of Bern as an attachment so you can see where the hotels are.
Call me when you arrive so we can arrange to meet. How about meeting for dinner instead of just a drink?
Looking forward to seeing you.
Bye for now
Johannes

Dear Sandy
Thanks for your email. You will find a good list of guest houses at the following address: www.berncityscope.ch/accommodation.htm. I think you can book online, which will save a lot of time. My parents stayed at Pension Bergland when they came to visit and I can recommend it. Alternatively, would you like me to book something for you?
Let me know what you decide.
All the best
Johannes

page 17

8
1. Just
2. quick
3. tell
4. for the
5. I'll
6. touch
7. tomorrow's
8. off
9. See you
10. Regards

Dear Mahendra
We are still waiting for the above order but have received no email to explain the reason for the delay. This is particularly inconvenient for us at the moment as ~~as~~ our clients need the delivery asap. Please can you contact the forwarders to find out what has happened and inform us immediately?
We look forward to hearing from you very soon.
Kind regards

Output
Speakers 1 and 4 think that mistakes in emails aren't that important.
Speakers 2 and 3 think they are important.
Speaker 5 thinks it depends on who you are writing to.

For more detail, see the Transcript on p. 59.

UNIT 3

page 18

Starter

H	capital 'h'	.	dot
h	small 'h'	@	at
-	hyphen/dash	/	slash
_	underscore	\	back slash

page 19

1 Suggested answers
Advantages:
- *Speed*: Emails are faster to write and send than letters or faxes.
- *Cost*: Emails are cheaper than sending letters or phoning.
- *Time to prepare*: The message is in writing so you can prepare what you want to say (particularly important when responding to #2).
- *Convenience*: A phone call can be inconvenient for the person being called, especially if he or she works at a busy place like a travel agency (#3). An email (or a letter or fax) can be answered at the recipient's convenience.

Disadvantages:
- *Accuracy*: In contrast to a phone call, you need to take care when writing an email (or a letter). Mistakes which may be overlooked on the phone could give a bad impression when in writing. The impression you make is particularly important when responding to #2 (job advert).
- You might get more detailed information with a phone call – especially with adverts #1 and #3 – as you can react to what the person says and ask follow-up questions.

2 Correct order:
4b 1d 3a 2c

Model emails
Dear Ms Karlsson
I saw your advertisement for the position of receptionist at the Hotel Falkenberg on the hoteljob.com website and am interested in applying for the job.
Could you please let me know if I can send my CV as an attachment or if you would prefer it by post?
Also, do I need to fill in an application form?
I look forward to hearing from you.
Regards

Dear Sir or Madam
I saw your advert in the Yellow Pages, and am interested in a holiday in Ireland next spring.
Could you please send me a brochure with tourist information and a list of accommodation?
My address is ...
I look forward to hearing from you soon.
Regards

page 20–21

3
1. Please answer asap.
2. Can you help?
3. Can you please send me ... ?
4. I'm sending you the ... in an attachment.
5. I'm sending you ...
6. Thanks for your email/request.
7. Let us know if you need any more help.
8. We hope you are happy with this.
9. Thanks for choosing ...
10. We are working on your request.

4
1. Could you please send
2. would you be able to help?
3. 'd (*or* would) appreciate a reply asap.
4. Thank you for your email.
5. your request is being processed.
6. in an attachment.
7. hope you find this satisfactory.
8. Thank you for your interest. / Do not hesitate to contact us if you require further assistance.

page 22

5 Model answers
Our general manager saw your advert in yesterday's Financial Times and would be grateful if you could send her the free start-up packet advertised.

Could you please send it to the following address?
...
We would also appreciate any information you can send us on your after-sales service.
Thank you in advance.
T. Gerald

Dear Giovanni
Jane at headquarters gave me your name and said you could help me. I need some information about the upcoming trade fair in Milan.
1) Who is attending from the Milan office?
2) How many hotel rooms have you booked?
3) What time and where is the Tuesday night reception?
Please send me the information asap.
Regards
Martin
PS Could you please give me your extension number? I can't find it on the international list.

6 2 request   5 send   8 know
3 asap   6 appreciate   9 interested
4 satisfactory   7 enquiry   10 receive

7 Model answer
To: James Baker
From: (*your name*)
Subject: after-sales service brochures/English

Dear James
I'm the sales rep for Bigtop electric drills and saws. Jane Miller gave me your name.
I am going to a trade fair in the Czech Republic next week and would like to order the English version of the after-sales service brochure. Could you please send me 1000 copies by Monday?
I would appreciate a reply asap.
Thank you for your help.
Regards
(*your name*)

page 23

8 Model answers
Dear Pia Stevens
Thank you for your enquiry about our 'progress' range of office furniture. The information you requested was sent by post this morning. It is also attached as a PDF file.
Please contact us if you need further assistance.
Regards

Dear Gérard Latour
Thank you for your email. The catalogue is in the post, and I have attached a list giving the addresses of all our stores so that you can see which is closest to you.
Please contact us if you need any more help.
Best wishes

page 24

Output
Scenario 1: You should delete the attachment.
Scenario 2: You should check with your friend that they really did send the email before opening the attachment.
1 You can install firewalls and buy virus protection software.
2 You shouldn't open attachments to emails from people you don't know. If you do know the sender, but the attachment looks suspicious, you should check with them first.
3 No; viruses have been a big problem since the early days of the Internet.

UNIT 4

page 25

Starter
1 thanks
2 thank you (or thanks) in advance
3 regarding
4 frequently asked questions
5 see you!
6 for your information
7 regards
8 by the way
9 forward
10 request
11 in my opinion
12 all the best

1 I'm looking forward to seeing you next week.
2 Thank you in advance for your help.
3 I will be in touch tomorrow with the updated figures.
4 Please call me regarding our meeting on Thursday morning.
5 This is just a quick email to give you the new dates.
6 Have you got any exciting plans for the weekend?
7 There is no information on pay rises at the moment. I hope to hear something soon, though.

page 26

1 1 He'd like them all to send him the figures from the last quarter by first thing the next morning. He'd also like Pascal to coordinate his team and send through their report (by Thursday 4th). Barbara should finish and send the sales report (by Tuesday 2nd June) and Thilo should contact Hungary about the new account details (as soon as possible).
2 Pascal has sent Simon the figures from the last quarter. He has also contacted his team and finished the sales figures. He hasn't finished the report as he and his team have been very busy.
3 They seem to have a good working relationship and their emails are informal and friendly, although Simon writes slightly more formally, possibly because he's the boss.

page 27

2 Barbara's reply:
d Sorry, Simon, but I haven't finished the report yet.
a Things have been so busy here that there hasn't been time to work on it.
c Tuesday should be no problem though.
b Last quarter's figures will be on your desk tomorrow a.m.

Thilo's reply:
- g Simon, Anna at the Hungarian office has just sent the account details.
- f I've put a copy in the post already, but am sending it as an attachment too.
- e I've also attached the figures that you wanted.

page 28

3
1. will be ('ll)
2. Have you ordered … yet
3. Have you contacted … yet
4. have you sent … yet
5. 've just ordered
6. 'll be delivered
7. 've just had a look
8. Have you seen
9. 'll forward
10. 've left
11. hasn't called back yet
12. 'll try
13. (will) ask
14. 'll email

4
arrange an appointment, a meeting
attach a document, the minutes, a report
clarify details
demand payment
finalize details, the minutes, a report
inform colleagues
meet colleagues, a deadline
notify colleagues
schedule an appointment, a meeting, payment
send details, the minutes, payment, a report
update a database
write the minutes, a report

page 29

1. sending
2. inform
3. arranged (or scheduled)
4. clarify
5. deadline
6. finalize
7. update
8. payment

5 The questions and requests might have been:
2. I'd be interested to know what you think.
3. Can you also send me the statistics on Internet use in the company, please?
4. I haven't heard from Sanji for ages. Have you?
5. Do you have the dates of the next internal policies meeting?

Model answer
Dear Martin
Could you send me a copy of the new Internet guidelines, please? I'd be interested to know what you think. Can you also send me the statistics on Internet use in the company, please?
BTW, I haven't heard from Sanji for ages. Have you? Any idea where she is?
One last thing – do you have the dates of the next internal policies meeting?
Many thanks!
Annika

page 30

6 Model answer
Dear Roger
I'm glad to hear the presentation went well.
First of all, Steve has agreed to do your presentation for you. I haven't corrected the overheads yet but will do so asap and give them to Steve.
Here's an update on what I've been doing while you've been away.
1) We've got an extension of 30 days from our suppliers.
2) I've booked a room at the International (the Hilton was not available) for the reception and have also received an offer for the buffet lunch. It's 50 euros a person. Is that OK?
3) I haven't renewed your parking permit yet but will do so by the end of the week.
4) Language courses have been arranged and I've informed the participants.
5) I haven't been able to reach Jeff yet (to cancel Friday) but I've left a message on his mailbox. I'll try again later.
6) Finally, I've spoken to Tessa about travel expenses, so that's OK.
Hope you have a successful meeting tomorrow.
All the best

page 31

Output
1. Over 160
2. Most are irrelevant to her work
3. Many decisions are confirmed in an email; not, as was previously the case, in a formal letter or memo.
4. Yes, because it enables him to know what's happening.
5. She'd like them to copy her in only once they've reached a conclusion.
6. She means 'not involve her in the discussion'.
7. She wants him to send her blind copies of everything and to send copies to other members of the team.
8. It means he has to spend a lot of time on emailing.
9. He thinks he isn't copied in on emails enough.
10. He'd like people to copy him in more.

UNIT 5

page 33

1
1. Mike introduces the email with the subject line, *Motorson invoice – the story continues!*. He then tells David he is giving him the low-down on the invoice to Motorson.
2. salutation: *Hi David*
informing: from *Here's the low-down …* to *what do you think?*
stating the action to be taken: *Could you call … ?*
giving a deadline: *I'll need the info by Friday 12th …*
close: *Cheers*

3 The humour in the subject line – *the story continues* – tells us that David already knows about the invoice. We also know that he already has a copy of the contract.
4 Mike has discovered that their contact person in the Finance Department has changed.
5 Mike asks David to call the company and find out the new details for the invoice, including who the new contact person is.

page 34

2
1 to look at sth in detail
2 to get in contact with sb
3 to send sth by post
4 to send sb an email
5 to give sb information
6 to try to find or get sth (that is missing)
7 to be out of touch or not have heard sth
8 to postpone sth (or put sth off)

Model answer
Hello Sally
Thanks for getting in touch and giving me the information/details on the March sales meeting. By the way, I called Barbara's office and tried to get the January figures but she's been on holiday – so no success there! Perhaps you could get in contact with Gary and ask him to send me an email with the info directly. I hope he can – I'd hate to have to postpone the meeting.
Oh, one last thing: can you send me a few of the new brochures. No hurry – the post will do!
Ciao
Jon

page 35

3
1 We'll report
2 We're happy
3 Let's introduce, They've been
4 plant's
5 haven't received, I'll send
6 Here's, we'll have to, it's not

4 1 b 2 d 3 c 4 e 5 a

page 36

5 Informing
Here are the details on …
I'm writing to clarify …
I'd like to inform you of …
Just a few comments about/on …
Just to update you on …
Let me fill you in on …
You'll find the info attached …

Replying
I'll get back to you asap …
Thank you for clarifying …
I'll follow up the points mentioned in your email …
Thanks for your email.

6
1 to update you on
2 get back to you asap
3 like to inform you of
4 the info attached
5 reply to your email
6 for your email
7 me fill you in on

page 37

7 Model answer
Bob
We have a slight problem. I asked you to send me the conference details *last week* but I still haven't received them. Unfortunately, the hotel needs the info today or we will lose the reservation. The situation is rather serious as this is the only hotel available in Madstown for our dates and I don't want to have to change the conference location. Could you please take care of this immediately? Thanks in advance.
Jack

page 38

8 Model answers
1 Hi Sira,
Just to let you know, the meeting is now on Wednesday (not Thursday as planned). Don't forget to bring the XS32 manual and a laptop!

2 Dear Pamela
Thanks for the update you sent. Yes, it's fine, but I still urgently need Manuel's travel plans. Please could you get them to me asap.
Also, I'll get back to you tomorrow with the new price list.
Thanks.

3 Hi John
Hope you had a good holiday!
To keep you updated: still nothing from Izumi about the Appleton account, but the Gantor-Brooks account has finally been approved.
If you can fit it in, I suggest a meeting with the two of us and Paul and Izumi next week. How about Thursday at 9.00? Let me know.

Output
1 He dislikes over-quoting: adding comments to a long email without deleting any of the previous message.
2 Because the recipient has to read the whole message again to find the original comments.
3 He recommends selecting the parts you are replying to and then deleting the rest. Also, he suggests changing the colour of replies (where this isn't done automatically).
4 Keep all email correspondence to one page or less and only quote relevant information.

UNIT 6

page 39

Starter
1 .com
2 ibm.de
3 .au
4 .at
5 .org
6 .ac.uk
7 .net
8 .ch
9 .ca
10 .gov
11 .es
12 .co.uk

1	.ie	Ireland	11	.cz	Czech Republic
2	.pt	Portugal	12	.sk	Slovakia
3	.fr	France	13	.ua	Ukraine
4	.it	Italy	14	.pl	Poland
5	.si	Slovenia	15	.by	Belarus
6	.al	Albania	16	.ee	Estonia
7	.gr	Greece	17	.se	Sweden
8	.tr	Turkey	18	.no	Norway
9	.hu	Hungary	19	.dk	Denmark
10	.at	Austria	20	.nl	Netherlands

page 40

1 **b** is the initial email, and **a** is the reply.
c is the initial email, and **d** is the reply.

page 41

2
1. arrange a meeting
2. arrange a time
3. How about
4. which time is convenient (for you)
5. we meet
6. pick you up
7. collect me/us
8. someone to collect me/us
9. confirm
10. convenient
11. to confirm this
12. Looking forward to

page 42

3
1. writing to arrange
2. What about
3. Is 12:30 OK
4. send me an email
5. to confirm
6. good for me
7. I look forward to

page 43

4
1. in
2. at
3. by
4. in
5. in
6. at
7. At, by
8. by, on

5 Model answer
Dear XXX
I am writing to arrange our second meeting to finalize the terms and conditions of the contract. I can suggest three possible times next week: Monday, 13 March at 2 pm, Thursday, 16 March at any time, or any time on Friday morning. I think we'll need about two hours to cover everything. Please let me know by tomorrow morning which date is most convenient for you. I need to reserve the conference room by noon.
Many thanks
Regards
YYY

6 Model answer
Dear YYY
Thanks for your email suggesting times for next week's meeting. I'd prefer to meet on Thursday at 2 pm if that's OK with you.
Please send me a quick email to confirm this. Looking forward to seeing you again.
Regards
XXX

page 44

7
1. I can't make …
   … later in the week is also impossible …
2. I'm afraid …

Sorry about this, …
3. Would it be all right with you if we postponed our meeting …
4. I should have time on …

8 Model answer
Hi Jason
Thanks for your email. I'm sorry to hear that we have to postpone the meeting. I'm afraid I can't make it on Tuesday, though. Could we meet at 9 am on either Wednesday or Friday instead?
Also, would it be all right if we met in my office and not at the café?
Please confirm the new date by Monday as I'll be out of the office all day Tuesday.
Best wishes
Marion

page 45

Output
1. Financial services, money-making schemes, medical equipment.
2. It's sent by companies gangs, and fraudsters. A lot comes from the US, China, Russia, and South Korea.
3. Don't reply to it; use a spam filter; don't open attachments; delete any mail from unknown senders.
4. Not always: spammers have ways of getting round them (e.g. by using images in attachments.)
5. 90 billion spam emails sent per day; Bill Gates receives around a million to his own email address.
6. Companies have to send you a link allowing you to unsubscribe.
7. Get a new address; only use it with people you trust; never register online; send individual copies. (All this advice would severely restrict your Internet use!)
8. One day, spam might completely saturate the Internet.

pages 46–47

Test yourself!

Across		Down	
2	deadline	1	hello
5	clarify	3	let me know
7	asap	4	by
10	spam	6	afraid
12	update	7	attachment
13	forward	8	at
15	touch	9	underscore
17	confirm	11	postpone
20	delete	13	FYI
21	just	14	assistance
22	reply	16	hold
23	grateful	18	re
27	make	19	please
28	dash	24	regards
29	dot	25	urgent
		26	hearing

A final tip for writing good, accurate emails:
Re-read it before you send it!

Transcripts

UNIT 1, OUTPUT

Interviewer They say these days that Big Brother is watching and reading your emails.
As more and more email is used at work, firms across America are growing concerned about what their employees are saying in company emails while on company time. According to a recent survey, about 45% of firms in the USA monitor their employees' electronic communication, including email, voice mail, and Internet use. And that figure is expected to rise.
For many of America's 78 million email users, this use of scanning equipment to monitor emails is too much like George Orwell's 'Big Brother'. But for the companies doing the monitoring, there are many good reasons for keeping an eye on their employees. I spoke to Bert Taylor, a Chicago-based consultant who advises companies on security and privacy issues. Bert, why do companies need to check on how their employees use email?

Bert Well, inappropriate email can really damage a company in a number of ways. Employees can send jokes which others might see as sexual harassment. Some emails can even reveal company decisions, which can later be used by the competition or even in court.

Interviewer And what about the effect of email use on people's time?

Bert Lost productivity isn't one of the main reasons for monitoring e-communication, but some firms are worried that workers spend too much time using computers as toys. 90% of workers say they receive personal emails during the working day.
Now many large companies are setting up policies on email and Internet use. For such policies to work, say experts, they must be in writing and they must be enforced.

UNIT 2, OUTPUT

Speaker 1 Writing emails is so easy! You don't have to worry about spelling, punctuation, or the order of the information! It's great. No need to check things. Just send.

Speaker 2 Hmm. I'm not sure you're right, you know. I've spoken to lots of native speakers and it really annoys them to receive mail with the wrong spelling and no punctuation. It looks as if you don't care.

Speaker 3 I agree. I get a lot of job applications and if the cover letter has too many mistakes I don't even bother opening the attached CV. Why would I want to hire someone who's sloppy and careless? And we do keep copies of email – they can never be completely deleted.

Speaker 4 Oh, come on. I think you're overreacting a bit. Email is supposed to be quick and who has time to check spelling and grammar? I think if the email is clear and understandable, who cares if there are a few, or even a lot of mistakes. Are capital letters and full stops that important?

Speaker 5 I think it probably depends who you are writing to. My close colleagues don't care if I make mistakes. Some don't even notice them. But if I'm writing to a customer or a supplier then I make sure my email is correct. After all, I don't want to give them the wrong impression.

UNIT 3, OUTPUT

Reporter Warnings of viruses – whether forwarded by friends or announced over the radio – have now become so common, it's difficult to know whether or not to take them seriously. Most companies play it safe and install so-called 'firewalls', which screen emails as they enter the system and prevent suspicious programs from infecting the computer network. You can also buy virus detection software, which can be updated from the Internet to protect PCs from viruses. However, neither of these precautions is 100% safe. I spoke to Alex Jackson, a computer security expert, and asked him what he recommends.

Alex The best advice is to be aware of viruses and to check emails carefully before opening them. If the email has no sender name, or contains attachments from people you don't know, it's best not to open them. Often viruses are unknowingly passed on, so you may receive an email from a colleague, but it has an unrelated attachment or an attachment with a strange name. In these cases, it's best to contact your colleague and ask what the attachment is before opening it.

Reporter Of course, computer viruses aren't a new phenomenon: in 1988 the 'Morris worm' virus infected nearly 10% of computers that had access to the Internet. Nowadays viruses are getting more sophisticated, though, so if your PC is used for emailing, it's best to be very careful and not open anything that looks suspicious.

UNIT 4, OUTPUT

Speaker 1 I get over 160 emails a day and most of them are totally useless. Just copies of emails to other colleagues, replies to those emails, comments on those replies, etc. etc. And most of the information has nothing to do with me. So, what's the point?

Speaker 2 I see your point but you shouldn't forget that a lot of decisions are made by email now. Things that used to be put into writing – and by that I mean official memos or formal letters sent by post – are now just being confirmed and recorded electronically. How many people do you know who actually print out their most important emails so there's a hard copy? If I didn't get copies electronically, I wouldn't know what's happening.

Speaker 3 I agree. I also get lots of emails where I've just been copied in. Maybe my colleagues are being nice to want to include me and not leave me out of the loop. But, let's face it, most of the time I don't really need the information. Particularly when there is a long email exchange between two colleagues. Wouldn't it be better just to copy me in (and the other ten people on the cc list) when they've reached a conclusion?

Speaker 4 My boss insists on getting blind copies of everything. I'm also supposed to cc every member of my team. I guess she wants to make sure that everyone has the same information and nobody has been left out. But it means I spend a lot of time going through my inbox.

Speaking 5 I don't know what you're all complaining about! I wish someone would cc me now and then! Nobody ever sends me copies of anything, even when the emails are about something I should know for my work. I wish this function were used more in our company.

UNIT 5, OUTPUT

Interviewer You were saying that some email habits annoy you?

Cecil Definitely. One thing which really irritates me is over-quoting. You know, when someone adds comments to a long email without deleting any of the previous message. This makes the recipient's job very difficult, as he or she has to read the whole message again to find the one or two short comments which were made.

Interviewer How can you avoid this?

Cecil Very simple. If there are several important points to reply to, select these sentences or paragraphs, insert your comments after them and delete everything else. You could even put your text in a different colour so it's clear which parts of the email are from the original message and which are your comments. (Most email programs do this automatically.)

Interviewer So don't send the whole thing back?

Cecil Never. If you leave the original message exactly as you received it and just add a quick comment to the top, it looks like you haven't really read the message. If I were writing a book on email etiquette, this would be rule number one: keep all e-correspondence to one page or less and only quote relevant information.

Interviewer Great. Thanks for the tip.

UNIT 6, OUTPUT

Presenter On today's programme we are looking at the menace of spam, emails you receive without asking from people offering you financial services, quick ways to make money, medical equipment, and so on. With me again is Alex Jackson. Alex, who is sending all this spam?

Alex Companies, gangs, fraudsters. All sorts of people.

Presenter And where are they based?

Alex This is very difficult to say but recent studies suggest the US, China, Russia, and South Korea are responsible for a lot of the world's spam.

Presenter And what happens if you respond to this sort of email?

Alex Well, first of all. It confirms to the sender that your email address is valid. This means you will get more and more spam as your address is passed on.

Presenter So, what is the best way to stop it?

Alex Spam filters are obviously good at detecting unwanted emails but the spammers are so clever that a lot still get past the filters. Spammers are using images as a way of getting past the filters since the filters are much better at spotting text. By clicking on the attachment you usually go to a website – most of which are in China apparently. Best advice is simply to delete any mail from anyone you are not sure about.

Presenter How large is the problem?

Alex It's growing every day. 90 billion per day according to recent studies. Apparently Bill Gates gets around a million a year to his own email address!

Presenter Can anything be done?

Alex Well, companies are obliged to provide a link for you to unsubscribe from mailing lists. But the huge numbers of unsolicited emails will carry on growing and might one day saturate the Internet completely. If you want to escape spam, get a brand new address, use it only with people you trust, never use it to register online and try to send individual rather than multiple copy emails. The problem is this will really restrict your use of the net!

Presenter Thanks very much Alex …

Useful phrases and vocabulary

The phrases on pages 61–63 are colour-coded according to how formal they are:

blue = more formal   **black = standard**   **green = (very) informal**

Please note that this is only an approximate guide. Whether a phrase is too formal or too informal often depends on the context of the email and your personal writing style.

Salutations

When you don't know the name:
Dear Sir or Madam
To whom it may concern
Hello
[no salutation]

When you know the name:
Dear Mr, Mrs, Ms …
Dear John
Hello Pat
Hi Mary
Hey John
Mira
[no salutation]

When writing to a group:
Dear all
Hi everyone

Opening sentence

Replying to an email:
Thanks (very much) for your email.
This is to say thanks for your email.

Giving a reason:
I'm (just) writing to …   clarify …
Just a (quick) note to …   confirm …
Just a short email to …   inform you…
                                follow up on …
                                let you know …
                                reply to …
                                request …
                                tell you …
                                thank you …
                                update you …

Attaching files

I'm sending you/attaching …
I've attached …
Please find attached …
I'm sending you the price list/document as an attachment.

When things go wrong:
I'm afraid you forgot to attach the file/…
I'm afraid I can't open the file/document. Can/Could you send it again in … format, please?

Making enquiries

I am interested in receiving/finding out …
I would like to receive …
We would be grateful if …
Could/Can you please send me … ?
Please send me …
Would you be able to (help) … ?
Can you help?
I'd appreciate a reply asap.
Please answer asap.

Replying to an enquiry

Thank you for your interest.
I'm pleased to send you …
I'm sending you … (in an attachment)
Please find the requested information attached.
We hope you find this satisfactory.
We hope you are happy/satisfied with this.
Thanks for choosing …

When there will be a delay:
Your request is being processed.
We are working on your request.

Informing

I'd like to inform you of …
Just a few comments about your last mail:
I'm writing to tell you about/let you know …
Just a note to say …
Here's the low-down on …
Just to update you on …
FYI: This is to let you know …
Hope this helps.
Let me/us know if you need anything else.

Requesting action

Have you … yet?
Can you send … to me by Friday, please?
I need … by Thursday.
Please get/keep in touch.
Keep me posted.

61

Useful phrases and vocabulary

Replying

Thanks for your email ...
In reply to your email, here are ...
Re your email, I ...
You'll find the info(rmation) attached.
I'll get back to you asap ...
I'll follow up the points mentioned in your email ...

Making arrangements

Just a quick note to arrange a time to meet.
I'm writing to set up/arrange ...
How/What about Tuesday?
Is ... OK?
Where should we meet?
Should I pick you up at/from ... ?
Could you collect me at ... ?

Confirming arrangements

I'd like to confirm ...
Just writing to confirm ...
Tuesday is good for me.
Please send me an email by 5 pm today to confirm this.
Looking forward to seeing/meeting ...

Changing arrangements

I'm sorry but I can't do/make Thursday.
This is to let you now that I've had to put off/postpone ...
I'm writing to call off/cancel ...
I'm afraid I can't make/manage Friday. How about ... instead?

Giving good news

I am/We are pleased to inform you ...
I'm happy to tell you ...
You'll be happy/delighted to hear that ...

Giving bad news

We regret to tell/inform you ...
I'm sorry, but ...
I am afraid that ...
Unfortunately, ...

Complaining

I'm writing to complain (about ...).
We're not happy with ...
I was disappointed to find/hear ...
I'm afraid that ...
Unfortunately, ...

Apologizing

For a delay in answering:
I do apologize for the delay in replying.
Sorry for the delay in getting back to you.
Sorry this is so late.

For not being able to help:
Sorry, I don't know.
I'm afraid I can't help you.

For something more serious:
We must apologize for ...
We deeply regret ...
My sincere apologies (*close*)
We apologize for any inconvenience caused.
Please accept our apologies.
I'm so sorry ...

Friendly ending

When you want a reply:
I look forward/Looking forward to hearing from you/to your reply.
Hope to hear from you soon.
I'd appreciate a reply asap.

Offering more help:
Do not hesitate to contact us if you need any assistance.
Feel free to get in touch ...
    if you have any other questions
    if you need more help.
    with any questions.
Let me know if you need anything else/if I can help you further.

General:
Thanks for your help/cooperation.
Hope all is well with you.
Have a nice day/weekend! :-)

Close

Yours sincerely
Kind/Best regards
Regards
Best wishes
All the best
Best
See you (soon)
Take care
Bye (for now)
[just the name or initials]
[no close]

Useful verbs (in context)

to apologize	I'd like to apologize for any inconvenience caused.
to appreciate	We'd appreciate a reply … /I'd appreciate it if you could send me …
to arrange	I'm writing to arrange a meeting … /Can you arrange for somebody to collect me …?
to ask (if)	Could I ask you to send me … ?/This is to ask if you could …
to assist	Please let us know if we can assist you in any way.
to clarify	I am writing to clarify the terms of the agreement.
to complain	I'm writing to complain about …/I'm afraid I must complain about …
to confirm	I'd like to confirm my booking/the date of our next meeting.
to contact	Please contact Mr … at our London office.
to enquire	I'd like to enquire about …
to follow up	Just wanted to follow up on that unpaid invoice.
to get in touch	Please get in touch (with me) asap.
to inform	FYI: This is to inform you that …/inform you of a problem …
to let sb know	Can you let me know the price of … ?/This is to let you know that we …
to need	I need those figures on my desk before tomorrow's meeting.
to postpone	I'm afraid we've had to postpone the conference.
to put off	Sorry, but we're going to have to put off the meeting till next week.
to receive	We've just received the invoice …
to regret	We regret to inform you that …
to reply	I am writing to reply to your enquiry about …
to send	We are sending you the handbook as an attachment.
to sort out	Please can you sort out the mess with the accounts!
to touch base	Just wanted to touch base with you before the meeting.
to update	This is to update you on the Johnson account.
to write	I'm writing to let you know …

Abbreviations and acronyms

Common abbreviations:

& (ampersand)	and	Jan	January
+	and/plus	Feb	February
ad(vert)	advertisement	Mar	March
am	in the morning	Apr	April
appt	appointment	May	May
asap	as soon as possible	Jun	June
at the mo	at the moment	Jul	July
eg	for example	Aug	August
etc	etcetera/and so on	Sept	September
ie	in other words	Oct	October
info	information	Nov	November
pls	please	Dec	December
pm	in the afternoon		
re	regarding/about	*Email, chatroom, and text-messaging:*	
rep	representative	FAQ	frequently asked questions
rgds	regards	Thx	thanks
w/e	weekend	TIA	thanks in advance
wk	week	IMO	in my opinion
yr	year/your	CU	see you
		FYI	for your information
Mon	Monday	BTW	by the way
Tues	Tuesday	Fwd	forward
Wed	Wednesday	LOL	laughing out loud
Thurs	Thursday	2	to
Fri	Friday	U	you
Sat	Saturday	RU	are you
Sun	Sunday		